101 WAYS TO CREATE AN UNFORGETTABLE CAMP EXPERIENCE

THE COLLECTION

This collection of summer camp program ideas came from the submissions of a few of the email round tables that are conducted monthly at SummerCampPro.com. These 101 program ideas were chosen because they are unique, creative and most can be done at either a day camp or resident (sleep-away) camp. These activities, programs and events were submitted by directors and program directors from all over the world.

EMAIL ROUND TABLES

Want to be part of future email round tables? Each month a new one is offered. Those on my email list get notified and have a few days to submit their ideas on the given topic. In return they are sent the complete compilation of everyone's ideas. This series of books are edited versions of those round tables. If you would like to participate in future email roundtable go to the home page of SummerCampPro.com and sign-up to receive email notifications.

Curt "Moose" Jackson
SummerCampPro.com

TABLE OF CONTENTS

ONGOING COMPETITIONS AND CHALLENGES

JUST FOR STAFF

OTHER

PART 1

SPECIAL PLACES

CREATING A MEMORABLE CAMP

Creating a memorable and magical place can happen in many ways at camp. While much of this can happen spontaneously in relational moments with staff and other campers, there is some director control in order to help create an environment that fosters that sense of wonder and excitement.

The things that can be controlled breakdown into four parts:
1. Create amazing programs, activities and experiences that are developed in such a way so that they are unique and fun, not a generic, cookie-cutter experience
2. Provide opportunities to grow and develop physically, mentally and spiritually
3. Using your facility and services to create special moments
4. Putting together a team of staff that are committed to making it all happen.

You are limited only by your imagination and creativity. The internet is a wonderful resource, but try to draw on past experiences and programs, books and the library as well, as they also house some awesome resources.

For planning an amazing event, there are two things that need to be worked out:
1. A detailed plan, including all components and how it is to be executed (Think Big! and include as many little details (i.e. costumes, theme, etc.) as possible)
2. Ensure that staff are provided full details on running the program and that you have enough staff to ensure the event is run properly and safely

THEMES

Following a theme is always a great thought, but when you take the theme to the extreme, it makes it all the more fun. For example, with a pirate theme you could create a theme meal around pirate food, build and race cardboard and duct tape boats between cabins (trust me I've done this and it always goes over well), design a treasure hunt etc.

These things are good and all tie into the theme, but what about having staff dress up in costume and make-up to bring real life character to the theme, create props and scenery that bring a certain amount of reality to it?

It's when you look at the details and try to bring them to life that really bring the sense of making a camp experience magical.

DAILY PROGRAM

With regards to daily program, the sense of magic can always be created as well. For example, in archery, kids will learn to shoot and have a good time, but what about having a staff member dress up as Robin Hood to teach it? Or during a high ropes activity, create a purpose, a reason for completing the challenge. Sometimes it's all too easy to placate ourselves and fall into running program that is rigid and repetitive.

Create, explore and imagine everything to be bigger and better.

STAFF

Most importantly, no amount of planning or creation will create wonder if you don't have the right staff to run the program and help create the experience for a camper. Staff will often make or break the success of an activity or program.

Over the years of working in various programs in a variety of roles, I've worked with staff that are incredibly committed and passionate to making camp an amazing place and staff that are there for the paycheck. Whenever possible, try to find staff that share a passion for making camp a magical place to be.

Easier said than done, though. I think the best way would be through your recruiting process. You could ask applicants something to the effect of, "If you were to come to camp in a staff position this summer, how would you make Camp _____ a more magical place to be?", either as perhaps an essay question on the application or as an interview question.

You could also work this into staff training by engaging staff in opportunities to run mock programs and role play.

These are all just suggestions, but really at the end of the day, camp is a memorable place all on it's own. The moments shared, the activities played, on their own create a sense of the magical. I've had campers and staff walk away changed, and I've walked away changed at the end of a session, and that is really what motivates me most.

To see kids be kids, to connect with other kids and staff in community and to see them achieve what they thought couldn't be done, and to grow as individuals. I still carry many fond memories from my years as camper, counselor and director, and wouldn't trade any of those experiences for the world.

SummerCampPro.com

POOH'S CORNER

We have a small hike along the lake our camp is on. We tell the youngest campers they are going to Pooh's house. Along the way they get to stop at Piglet's house and go inside (it's a tree that a neighbor hollowed out and put a latter in so you could see out the top). When they get to the end of the hike there is a table made out of rocks and a few seats. Pooh, though is always busy, but he leaves a note explaining his absence along with some snacks.

Instead of Pooh's Corner you could set up areas, or scenes, from other books:
- Tea Time with Alice in Wonderland
- The Giving Tree
- Dr Seuss' Secret Hideaway
- The New Order of the Phoenix Hideout
- The Magic Tree
- Where the Wild Things Are
- Where the Moose makes his muffins
- The cabin of the Three Bears that Goldilocks visited
- The Bridge to Terabithia
- The Shire
- Grandma's Cabin that Red-Riding Hood visits

MYSTERY TRIP

Our camp is a traveling summer camp, which means we take a field trip every day. While that sounds exciting, the campers (and staff) begin to get a little bit jaded towards the end of the summer after visiting the same places again and again.

A while back we instituted a Mystery Trip. The trip is towards the end of the week, which enables me to give out clues in the days leading up to the trip.

For example, the older group's Mystery Trip was going to this really cool movie theater / restaurant. Their first clue was a chicken (I had pre-ordered chicken fingers and French fries for everyone). The second clue had something to do with a couch potato. You could also have them complete a daily challenge to get their clue.

No one in the entire camp knew where the Mystery Trips were to. The campers and counselors had all sorts of crazy ideas and theories, even going as far as to predict what their next clue would be, and what it could mean.

By mid-week, everyone was very excited about the clues, their guesses and the whole mystery idea. Parents were even stopping me in the hallway to ask questions and were shocked when I wouldn't tell them!

THE TWILIGHT CAFE

At the end of each evening of our daily summer "Twilight Camp", the staff and campers sit and enjoy The Twilight Café; a circle of friends enjoying their choices of (and inventions of) a variety of hot drinks and reviewing their time together that day.

The campers are invited to bring along their own favorite cup/mug while the counselors heat water for the drink mixes. Drink mixes include the usual, as well as all colors of Jello, herbal teas, and occasionally whipped cream and sprinkles.

It's a calming end to what may have been a sweaty beach hike or intense game of forest capture-the-flag, and it brings the group together to reflect on their camp experience before parents arrive for pick up.

This age group (11-13) really enjoys the "grown up-ness" of the café after being loud and goofy at camp.

If you want to create your own Twilight Cafe Here are some suggestions:
- Find a spot that is comfortable and away from the rest of camp.
- Create some comfortable seating using a combination of things like couches, oversized chairs, cushions, a rug, coffee tables, etc. Of course, just some regular chairs and tables will do the trick as well.
- Put on some calming music at a low volume.
- Have hot water available.
- Provide a variety of teas and hot cocoa.
- Consider have light snacks or fruit available.
- Each day you could have a special juice or smoothie available. If so, have a blender or two ready.

SECRET STONES

At one camp there is a tradition that the last week of each session, all campers are lead to Skull Rock by the Site Director (no one knows how it got its name, it's a large rock in the middle of a large wooded area in camp). The kids love this, as it is the only time they are taken to the rock and they really look forward to going.

At another camp there is a huge rock that has a flat surface on top. The surface is large enough to seat 20 campers. It's called Storybook Rock. Counselors take their groups to the rock and tell, or read, a story of their choosing. Stories range from camp lore to Native American parables.

At yet another camp, there is a place that looks like a bunch of boulders had been stacked together. It's a wonderful place for kids to climb around and on top of. Counselors take their groups to this special spot for devotions and serious talks about life. Groups get to visit only once per session.

Is there a huge rock or boulder around your camp that can be a special place for groups to visit? If so, create a story around it. Take group pictures there. Create a box that houses a binder where campers who visit can leave their names and thoughts in. Hide a toy or action figure somewhere in the cracks for a camper to discover. you can do all sorts of neat things at a place like this.

LETTING GO

Nearly everyone has a burden of some sort. It could be big or it could be small. Some are good and some are not. The burden of motherhood can be a wonderful thing. The burden of friendship as well. However, the burden of keeping a dark secret or the burden of jealousy are not things we want in our life. The burden of living up to our parent's expectations or the guilt of wronging someone in our life are other examples of burdens we don't want.

One way to unburden our lives is by sharing that problem with someone else. Camp is a place where a camper or staff person might be able to do that. If you speak to your group of campers about what a burden is and how we can cope with burdens you could be changing lives.

But sometimes we just cannot bring ourselves to share our burdens with others. That's where the following idea comes in. It's an idea that comes from a very special camp in California.

Away from camp a fair distance, an old tree has been made into a monument by older campers. It is decorated with branches and flowers the first day. It has a poem on it that says "our lives are filled with joy and pain. Our share of sun our share of rain" and goes on to invite them to leave a stone representing a burden that they are ready to let go of.

If you had the campers and counselors carry a decent sized rock from a good distance over to the tree it would be a great metaphor for the burdens we carry and how we want to get rid of them because they can be too heavy for us over time.

FAIRY VILLAGE

At my camp there is a place in the woods (still on camp property but hard to find) that is off the trail. It's a fairy village that is 5 summers in the making.

Currently there are 32 fairy houses. They all look different and are made from different materials. Each one has a story, though. Every summer the camp staff is given the opportunity to create a fairy house and add it to the village. Obviously, not everyone is going to participate in building this fairy community we have going. However, those that do really seem to get into it.

Counselors love to take their groups to see the village. We ask any staff that want to visit the village with their group to take a special route, instead of a direct route, so that the campers cannot find the village on their own. Once they are at the village the counselors talk about how the fairies are out exploring during the day, which is why we don't see any, or perhaps it's because they can hear us coming and they choose to hide. Nobody really knows. The campers, especially the younger ones, are usually in awe. Each week we get campers begging to visit the fairy village.

We are considering allowing our oldest campers (high school) and/or CITs the chance to create a fairy house.

The houses are created with rocks, sticks, leaves, pine cones, brush, shells, acorns, and anything else that can be found in nature. Glue is used to keep everything together if needed. We want the houses to last a very long time. Some staff have created shops as well, like the "Wing Repair" shop, "Pixie Dust" shop, grocery store, general store, and others.

Other materials, besides what nature provides, has been used in the creation of the houses and shops as well, including mason jars, bird houses from a craft store, yarn, string, wire, fake moss, spray paint, doll furniture, sequins, ghourds, Legos, and even a fake pumpkin.

We have a fairy village scrapbook. Each page has a picture of the fairy house (or shop) along side a picture of the staff person who created it. We also write in the year it was created.

WISHING AREA

Our camp used to have a working well many years ago. Well before I got here. After the original owners stopped using it staff turned it into a "wishing well". Campers and staff would toss coins in the well and make a wish.

Years late the wishing well was removed by new owners of the camp. They hadn't realized what they'd done until the summer came around and staff and campers were outraged. This long standing tradition had been destroyed.

The new owners got together with some of the staff to brainstorm a solution. They decided to use an area where there was a little waterfall that fell into the beginning of a creek. It already had the legend of being a magical place. So they decided to play on that lore and create a "wishing area".

That is not the story we tell the campers, of course. Only a few of the leadership staff know the trued story above. Instead we have a long story about how the area became a magical place that had the power to grant wishes to those who have a pure heart. The wishes cannot be self serving and those wanting to make a wish must find the perfect stone to toss into the waterfall.

The story about how it became magical is a camp secret so I cannot share it here. However, any camp can find there own "wishing area". Find a spot that is secluded and has a magical feel to it. Then create a legend for the area, a magical history. After that decided on a special way campers must make their wish. We use rocks, but it can be just about anything.

PART
2

DECORATIONS

STAFF LANTERNS

Every Thursday night, we have a traditional all-camp campfire with inspirational stories, a few of our beloved slow-paced campfire songs, (complete with guitar accompaniment) and a telling of the history and legends specific to our camp.

During this night, we also have lanterns lit across the stage of the campfire area. Each staff member makes a lantern at the beginning of the summer, and each Thursday night, they are illuminated with a candle. At the end of the campfire, the entire staff comes on the main stage, sings a song, and units are dismissed one at a time. The staff members who live in the dismissed unit pick up their lanterns, gather their campers, and lead the way back to the unit by the light of the lantern.

We introduce the idea of the lanterns with an all-staff campfire during staff training which mimics the real thing. The leadership staff has their lanterns made and lined up around the stage, and the campfire functions as if the leadership staff was the camp staff, and the camp staff was the campers. The next day during staff training, we plan time for the rest of the staff to make their lanterns.

Making the Lanterns

Several years ago, we built a greenhouse made of recycled 2-liter soda bottles, and we find piles of leftover bottles everywhere. Our lanterns are made from the 2-liter soda bottles.

Supplies:
- 2-liter soda bottles
- Tissue paper
- Glue
- Exacto knife
- Whole punch
- Wire

Instructions:
1. Remove any labels on the bottles.
2. Cut off the top 1/3 off the two-liter soda bottle with the exacto knife, and set aside.
3. Hole-punch two holes at the top of the bottle across from each other (the holes are for stringing a wire handle through later).
4. Pour some Elmer's glue in a bowl and add some water (for a cup of glue add a little less then 1/8 cup of water). The glue should be just a little thinner than normal.
5. Use this glue mixture to paste tissue paper (cut it, rip it, anything you want) on the outside of the bottle to decorate.
6. When the glue dries, attach the wire through the holes to make a handle.

Optional: The top of the bottle can be placed inside the bottom, upside down. This creates a sort of platform in the middle of the bottle to keep the candle from being on the very bottom of the bottle. It also makes the lantern double-layered, and a little sturdier. The downside of this optional adjustment: the curved surface of the top of the bottle can be difficult to place a candle on.

LUMINARIA

On the last night of each session, we create a path to the campfire with paper lanterns made of paper bags and tea lights. It is really beautiful and creates a really great energy because the campers know that something special is happening.

Make sure that you add some pebbles or dirt to the bottom of each paper bag so it doesn't blow away.

As an example of what it can look like here is a photo from www.party-ideas-by-a-pro.com.

You can place the bags a foot apart or four feet apart. It all depends on the look you want and how many you can make and place. fake tea lights are safe and can be used over and over. I find that the best places to purchase them are at a dollar store, Target, WalMart, or Amazon.com.

BALLOONS

A quick and easy way to create a festive and fun environment is with the use of balloons. Many times we use a few balloons to highlight things like the registration table or a birthday. We can do so much more than that with balloons.

We try to have balloons lining our road into camp at least 2x week. If we have a dress up day, like for the Orioles, we'll post Black and Orange balloons. Israel Day gets Blue and White ones. Color war- well, that's obvious. They just lend to a fun atmosphere. Instead of getting the small helium tank from a party store, find out who in your area supply's oxygen. It is worth it for the festive atmosphere.

The more there are, or the bigger they are, the better. Check Google or Pinterest for some great ideas on decorating with balloons. Here are a few ideas:

- Arches
- Dining room tables
- Tie into flowers and put in vases
- Tie into animals
- Make designs using chicken wire
- Match color to theme
- Balloon columns
- Combine with streamers
- Combine with glow sticks

DECORATING YOUR SPACE

A day or two before camp begins, the counselors come to camp and decorate their space. This can be their cabin, their room, their area of the gym, etc.

They pick a bunk/room/area name that corresponds with our theme and they decorate the walls and door from top to bottom accordingly. (They pretty much make all of their decorations with bulletin board paper, so it costs next to nothing.) When the campers walk in on the first day, the decorations sweep them right into the camp spirit.

It's nice to have the office staff decorate the office, the kitchen staff decorate the dining hall, the specialty staff decorate their activity areas, etc. Decorations all over camp add to the magic of camp. Don't forget that there are other things that can be decorated, including the camp vans, the campfire area, the front of camp, the maintenance shed, the Gaga Pit, the sailboats, the camp store, etc.

You can use:
- bulletin board paper
- butcher paper
- poster board
- streamers
- balloons
- fabric
- shower curtains
- cardboard
- ribbon
- bows
- netting
- fake vines, etc.

Dollar stores and thrift shops are great places to find inexpensive decorating items.

PICTURES AROUND CAMP

Something we found to be fun and memorable was posting different types of posters around camp. The posters change pretty often and there is a variety of them. The campers and staff get a kick out of them and often have suggestions for others. Here are some that we have done.

WANTED POSTERS

We'll take pictures of a staff members in western clothes and create Wanted Posters. One may say "Wanted Dead or Alive $1,000,000 bounty", and another may say, "Wanted Dead or Alive $.25 bounty". The campers think it's so funny that one of the staff members has a bounty of a quarter out for them.

FOUND POSTERS

We saw a found poster of a velociraptor. It was very funny. So, we decided to play off that and create found posters of other things from movies like:

- Buttercup - Prim's cat from the Hunger Games
- Boo - the little girl from Monster's Inc.
- Nemo - from Finding Nemo
- A pair of goggles that came from a Minion - from Despicable Me
- Ruby Slippers - from Wizard of Oz
- Captain America's shield
- R2-D2 - from Star Wars

MISSING (LOST) POSTERS

We also put up missing posters. We saw a "Lost Ring" poster (Lord of the Rings) that inspired us to make our own.

- Camp Mascot which is a stuffed animal
- Waldo - from Where's Waldo
- Record player for the camp dance
- Invisible Jet - Wonder Woman

BULLETIN BOARD ADS

These are the posters that have the little strips of paper you can pull off. Again, we got inspiration from Pinterest and Google Images.

- FREE Compliments - each strip of paper had a compliment
- FREE Strips of paper - nothing was on the strips

CAMP PLAQUES

I firmly believe in camp traditions. One of the many I started was after seeing this done at my first camp. We created camp plaques. Each session, every cabin group was given a 4 in circle or square to create a plaque decorated anyway they would like. It had to say year, session, and cabin (i.e. 2014, A2, Session 2). We then attached them around the Dining Hall wall and rafters.

After I left 10 years later, the walls were covered with memories. Staff, campers and alumni were always looking for theirs. Something so simple allowed people to leave their mark in a place they care about.

There are other sizes and shapes of plaques that can be used for the same purpose.

PART

3

CEREMONIES

A SPECIAL CEREMONY

This is a good one to do with staff or your oldest campers (CIT, Teen Leaders, or whatever you call them at camp…). It does take a bit of preparation but it's totally cool!

Set-up:
- Depending on the number of people you'll need a handful of GLOW STICKS, any color works.
- Being very, very careful, cut open the glow sticks. You don't want to disrupt the glass tube in the middle (yet).
- Pour the liquid from your open glow sticks into a container. WASH YOUR HANDS
- Now break open the glass tubes from the middle of the glow sticks.
- Pour the liquid into another container. WASH YOUR HANDS
- Be very careful not to contaminate either of the containers with the liquid, otherwise they will start to glow too soon.

Activity:
Works best at night, but any dark space will work
- Have your staff/campers stand in a circle or make two lines facing a partner.
- With your two containers you want one partner to put a finger (or two) in one of the solutions while the other person dips into the other (or every other person if standing in a circle).
- Then give a special speech on the power of working together – there are many of them out there, you pick which one works best for your camp. I always end with "that by ourselves we can accomplish a lot… now touch your partner's fingers (and they should glow)…but together we can accomplish so much more".

Adapt to fit your ceremony. It's really neat and if they have never done it before they are blown away by it. Do remind them to wash their hands and not to get it on clothes. It'll stain clothes and it's probably not good to eat! A little does go a long ways. With a staff of 30 I used about 4 glow sticks.

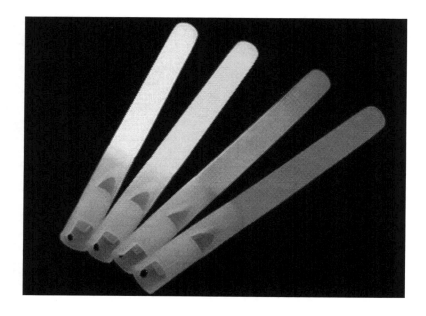

CREATING A FRATERNITY

One of the most moving things I have ever seen at camp, is a brotherhood through building a Fraternity based on motivation, mutual respect and support for one another. The teens were extremely into the idea, and they were able to overcome fears and build friendships with the help of this brotherhood.

On the first night, a ceremony was held inside a dark cabin, where the Fraternity expectations were laid out by the counselors. At a table that was lit with only candles, the boys were asked to sign a pact.

Every one was given a strip of a bandana, which was tied around the wrist to signify their membership. (Each person possessing a bandana piece signified being a part of something larger than themselves.)

Throughout the week, the boys were reminded to live up to the pact. (Being a "Gentleman" was also emphasized, if the boys were to impress the girls and ask them to the dance at the end of the week!)

Every night before bed, the Fraternity met to review the day. A focus question was posed each night; examples included "What is something you did today that you had not done before?" and "Thank some one in the room for something they have helped you do this week." During these review sessions, the boys were very sincere and even started crying over the accomplishments they had made in a week's time.

At the last Cabin meeting, every one was give a cardboard paddle that had the Fraternity crest, camp, year and Superlative Award that they earned ("Most Courageous," etc.). A piece of the bandana was also tied to the top.

The counselors did a great job of emphasizing that the Fraternity was built on strength, respect and support, while also having fun. (There weren't any pranks or hazing events.) Both the staff and the counselors left the week with a different perspective about life.

GRADUATION FROM CAMP

For the last 15 years, we have been celebrating our campers as they graduate from camp. We assign the last day of sr. high camp to create a special grad day.

We start off with a sleep in and a fun breakfast theme, maybe breakfast in bed or cartoon breakfast, and have a relaxed day of programming, more of a choice day. For lunch we have a special outdoor BBQ with music, and then in the afternoon we transform our dining hall into a banquet hall and our basement into a coffee house. We allow any campers that want to help set up and decorate to do so.

Campers are told before they arrive that the grad is happening so they can bring special clothes if they like. We start with appetizers out side and we take photos, then we move inside for the banquet. After dinner we set up a coffee house and dessert buffet. Campers have time to change before we start if they like. We serve special coffees, drinks and desserts before we start and at intermission.

The entertainment is from the staff and campers who have signed up during the week. We present grad certificates to our graduating campers and film the whole evening and make a special coffee house DVD for purchase. We end with an amazing campfire time, just celebrating the week.

Below is a bit of a checklist for the prep work:

FRIDAY, Sr High – Grad & Coffee House

Staff Meeting:
- Have staff each blow up 5-ish balloons
- Assign non-counseling staff roles (set up, serving, etc)
- Pick songs for chapel and campfire
- Remind activity instructors: some may opt out of last block to help with setup

8:30 Star Wars Breakfast
- Big Star Wars decorations
- Star Wars goodie bags
- Take volunteers for basement setup – sign up for afternoon activity block or free-time

9:00 Cabin Clean-up and BBQ setup
- BBQ's ready to go - matches, firestarter
- Set up tables for food, with tablecloths
- Pop cooler – fill with ice & pop
- Sound System & good tunes

Dining Hall setup:
- Move tables, put out tablecloths & candles

10:30 Activity #1 and Start BBQ @ 11

11:20 Activity #2 and Start BBQing @ 11:45

12:15 BBQ Lunch

1:00 Coffee house setup: (to be done during activity block & free-time, with camper help)
- Bring in tables and chairs, cushions and couches
- Set up sound system
- Get coffee house stuff together and ready to go (poster, cups, coffee machine, other ingredients)
- Do coffee house beverage prep – syrups, grinding, etc
- Cover table
- Crayons on tables
- White lights
- Grad certificates and gifts
- Camp video: projector, screen, DVD player

1:45 Activity #3

2:30 Free-Time

4:20 Grad Prep

5:05 Hors D'oeuvres & Pictures
Servers:_____, _____, _____, _____,

- Cabin Photos and other photos (take orders):

6:00 Grad Dinner Banquet
- Coffee house prep – start coffee and water, etc.
- Set up coffee and dessert station
Post-dinner:
- Send campers to change, get ready for entertainment
- Bring all desserts and beverage items down – support staff help
- Light candles

7:15 Coffee House
- Music on sound system when people come in
- Desserts and coffee (round 1)
- Entertainment
- Desserts and coffee (round 2)
- Entertainment
- Grad and LIGHT certificates
- Camp Video

9:30 Campfire

LIT PROGRAM 'GRADUATION'

At the end of the LIT program (which runs parallel to the camper program during the camper week) we hold a little ceremony for our LIT's who have completed their program.

On the last night of camp we have all of the campers and staff stand in two lines, facing each other with the LIT's standing in the middle (on the camper side, just in front of the younger campers) with an unlit candle.

The LIT director does a little speech about their years as campers, and all of the new skills and experiences we hope they take away from the LIT program.

We then ask them to step over towards their counselor who light their candles. (All the counselors already had lit candles) once their candle was lit, we asked them to turn around and face the other campers (they would now be on the counselor side of the line).

Then the LIT director tells them that even though they aren't going to be campers anymore, they will always be part of the camp family and hopefully they will use the skills and lessons they've learned as campers and LIT's to influence a younger generation of campers the way that their counselors have influenced them, to "pass the torch" so to speak.

It's a very emotional ceremony, and really solemn and beautiful if done right.

LAST NIGHT CEREMONY

Our camp is held at a State Park group camping facility that was built by the CCC, so there is a lot of history and magic just in our location. One of the traditions that campers remember for years and years is the ceremony we do on the last night of camp at campfire time.

Each camper and counselor takes a stick, walks up on the hearth of our massive outdoor fireplace, throws the stick on the fire and tells everyone the thing they liked best about camp. There have been some truly touching thing shared, lots of funny stories, and some that were a little awkward, but it is a memorable time.

After everyone, including counselors and staff, have shared their story, we walk around the outside and stand until everyone is done. We then hold hands and sing the song, "Make new friends and keep the old, one is silver and one is gold. A circle's round and has no end, that's how long I want to be your friend."

WATERBUGS and DRAGONFLIES

We have several traditions and ceremonies at camp. We're a children's oncology camp, so we try to focus on the survival/life side instead of the death portion of cancer, but it is necessary to acknowledge both sides.

On Tuesday morning, we gather together at our campfire for a memorial ceremony to remember our friends who have lost their battle by reading "Waterbugs and Dragonflies" by Doris Stickney. This is a story than can be told to any child who is struggling with the idea of death.

Waterbugs and Dragonflies: Explaining Death to Young Children
Down below the surface of a quiet pond lived a little colony of water bugs. They were a happy colony, living far away from the sun. For many months they were very busy, scurrying over the soft mud on the bottom of the pond. They did notice that every once in awhile one of their colony seemed to lose interest in going about. Clinging to the stem of a pond lily it gradually moved out of sight and was seen no more. "Look!" said one of the water bugs to another. "One of our colony is climbing up the lily stalk. Where do you think she is going?" Up, up, up it slowly went....Even as they watched, the water bug disappeared from sight. Its friends waited and waited but it didn't return...

"That's funny!" said one water bug to another. "Wasn't she happy here?" asked a second... "Where do you suppose she went?" wondered a third. No one had an answer. They were greatly puzzled. Finally one of the water bugs, a leader in the colony, gathered its friends together. "I have an idea". The next one of us who climbs up the lily stalk must promise to come back and tell us where he or she went and why."

"We promise", they said solemnly.

One spring day, not long after, the very water bug who had suggested the plan found himself climbing up the lily stalk. Up, up, up, he went. Before he knew what was happening, he had broke through the surface of the water and fallen onto the broad, green lily pad above. When he awoke, he looked about with surprise. He couldn't believe what he saw. A startling change had come to his old body. His movement revealed four silver wings and a long tail. Even as he struggled, he felt an impulse to move his wings...The warmth of the sun soon dried the moisture from the new body. He moved his wings again and suddenly found himself up above the water. He had become a dragonfly!!

Swooping and dipping in great curves, he flew through the air. He felt exhilarated in the new atmosphere. By and by the new dragonfly lighted happily on a lily pad to rest. Then it was that he chanced to look below to the bottom of the pond. Why, he was right above his old friends, the water bugs! There they were scurrying around, just as he had been doing some time before.

The dragonfly remembered the promise: "The next one of us who climbs up the lily stalk will come back and tell where he or she went and why." Without thinking, the dragonfly darted down. Suddenly he hit the surface of the water and bounced away. Now that he was a dragonfly, he could no longer go into the water...

"I can't return!" he said in dismay. "At least, I tried. But I can't keep my promise. Even if I could go back, not one of the water bugs would know me in my new body. I guess I'll just have to wait until they become dragonflies too. Then they'll understand what has happened to me, and where I went."

And the dragonfly winged off happily into its wonderful new world of sun and air.......

From: "Waterbugs and Dragonflies : Explaining Death to Young Children" by Doris Stickney

After the story, we remind our campers what cancer cannot do with the following poem:

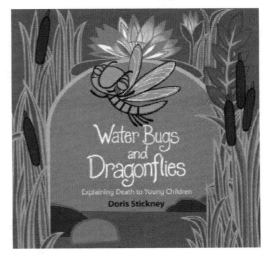

What Cancer Cannot Do
Cancer is so limited....
It cannot cripple love.
It cannot shatter hope.
It cannot corrode faith.
It cannot eat away peace.
It cannot destroy confidence.
It cannot kill friendship.
It cannot shut out memories.
It cannot silence courage.
It cannot reduce eternal life.
It cannot quench the Spirit.

We call out the names of our friends who have earned their wings and recite a poem: "We Remember Them"

We Remember Them
In the rising of the sun and its going down, We Remember Them.
In the bowing of the wind and in the chill of winter, We Remember Them.
In the opening of the buds and in the rebirth of spring. We Remember Them.
In the blueness of the skies and in the warmth of summer, We Remember Them.
In the rustling of the leaves and in the beauty of autumn, We Remember Them.
In the beginning of the year and when it ends, We Remember Them.
When we are weary and in need of strength, We Remember Them.
When we are lost and sick of heart, We Remember Them.
When we have joys and special celebrations we yearn to share, We Remember Them.
So long as we live, they too shall live, for they are part of us. We Remember Them.
-From the Jewish Book Of Prayer

On the way out of the ceremony, the campers and counselors hang ornaments that they have made on our remembrance tree where they remain the rest of the week. After the memorial, we usually send the kids straight off to an uplifting activity to move along with the real reason we're at camp: surviving and making the most out of life. Some campers (and counselors) need some extra time and support, which is of course provided.

INDIAN TRADITION

I am from India. Here is an activity that I do regularly.

We Indians are keen on traditions and rituals. On our birthday, we always bow to the elders and they give us their blessings. However, this small gesture in the form of a ritual would add colour and make the kids feel important.

If any of the kids have their birthday during the camp days, we arrange for some flower petals the previous evening. (The birthday boy/girl wouldn't know about it.) When that child enters the class, or when he just steps in, we shower the petals on him, either from a height, like someone standing on a chair, or we hide behind the door, and when he steps in, the petals are showered on him.

This makes the child feel very important, and he wears a happy smile the whole day long. The smell and touch of flower petals gives a feeling of joy...this could also be done on the first day to welcome the kids.

Cultural traditions can be an important part of camp. What do other cultures do for birthdays? How can you incorporate those into your camp program?

Now that's a lot of flower petals!

A BIRTHDAY CHOICE

At our camp, we do something very memorable for campers celebrating their birthday with us.

The camper comes and stands on a seat, and then the counselors of the opposite gender come and kneel down all around the camper like they are proposing. With outstretched arms each of them lift an object of some sort as an offering to the camper while they sing a very heartfelt rendition of Happy Birthday.

It looks hilarious and over the years the items have gone from weird to weirder, and bigger (like a fake tree that sits in the dining hall). The campers love seeing what the counselors will choose for their object to sing with, while the birthday camper is trying not to laugh at all the ridiculous objects being held towards him/her.

SAYING GOODBYE

The purpose of this ritual is to help the campers say goodbye to one another and to camp. One version of this ritual follows.

The night has fallen and the camp is completely quiet. A small procession of leaders in robes walks by each cabin/tent. If you have horses, they could be on horseback. As they do, the campers and counselors silently file in behind them. If the camp isn't well lit, some people can carry lanterns (preferably not flashlights) or torches.

Once everyone has been gathered at a special location, the camp walks in a circle and people sit on benches or the ground in a circle – usually several nested circles. In the middle is something resembling a large wedding cake – several tiers with a wide base and smaller, higher levels. The structure is just wood planks, sometimes decorated.

All lights are put out and everyone sits in silence for a moment – sometimes with a thought to think about. Then, one person lights a candle (everyone has a candle) and passes the flame along until everyone's candle is lit. By cabin groups, campers and counselors place their candles on the structure. This usually makes for a very bright area.

Songs are sung and groups sometimes make short speeches. Remembrances are often spoken or read. Then the campers are given time to say goodbye to one another. As that is taking place, the candles are slowly being put out one by one.

When the last candle is out, everyone must be silent and go back to their cabin. The next morning everyone leaves to go home.

SummerCampPro.com

BURNING PHOENIX

Our camp season ended with our directing staff (all three of us) constructing a giant wooden and hay-filled phoenix which was burned to symbolize the end of the season and the wait for its rebirth next season.

We allowed our top archers to fire flaming arrows at it after it was lightly sprayed with a flammable fluid (which I assume was diesel gasoline) and it made for a great spectacle for the staff and campers' final night at the camp.

There was also a special ceremony before it was burned where we said a devotion while each camper placed 2 sticks in the heart of the phoenix with wishes attached to them. One stick had a selfless wish and the other was a wish for humanity (also selfless, but not stated).

R.I.P. MEAN WORDS
Staff find a small cardboard box and write 'Hate Casket' and/or 'RIP Mean Words' etc., on it.

At our youth leadership camp, early in the second day, we gave each participant and staff a half piece of paper and a pencil and asked them to write two types of 'mean words' (sentences) on the page.

1. Words that they regret having said to someone else
2. Words that someone else has said to them that made them feel badly, hurt their feelings, etc.

Once they are done, campers and staff are asked to fold the paper in half and place it in the casket. Staff ask the campers and their coworkers to think about what they wrote down, and reflect during the rest of the day about what impact those mean words have had on them or the victim of their own mean words.

In the early evening before it was too dark, we lit our campfire and brought the casket out. One staff handed out the pages from the hate casket, giving one to each camper and staff.(randomly, not the one they wrote).

Each person reads the page they are handed, and once they have completed the reading, puts the refolded page back into the casket. (a staff stands beside campers when they read, in case they need help, and to have the casket available for the pages to be placed in.)

After all of the mean words are read, staff conduct a debrief about some of the content of the letters. The depth of the debrief would depend on the training/education/skill level of the staff.

After the debrief, staff place the hate casket in the fire and ask campers to commit to avoiding using the mean words that have been burned.

For the rest of the week, we heard the campers make comments to each other like 'We burned those words', when negative situations occurred. This is one of the most powerful exercises I have witnessed at this camp over the years.

PART
4

MEALS

THEME MEALS

Theme meals are very memorable. It doesn't have to be just for dinners, either.

Here are some camper favorites:

BREAKFAST
- Cartoon Breakfast - For this breakfast campers and staff can wear their PJs. We have a contests for the best bed head, PJs, and one for the best cartoon impression. During the meal we show clips of different cartoons on a projector.
- Cereal Mayhem - During this meal staff dress up as different cereal characters (Count Chocula, Cap'n Crunch, the Trix Rabbit, etc. We have all the costumes in our storage. We also have available just about every cereal you can imagine available.

LUNCH
- Super Hero Spread - Lunches get looked over much of the time when it comes to theme meals. Not with us. In fact, many time lunches are the best theme meals we run. With Super Hero Spread we decorate and dress the part. I think the decorations are the main attraction since we go all out on this one. For food we have Sup-er Salad (Soup or Salad). We set out a variety of soups and really go to town with the available salad toppings. The tables all have super hero trivia that the counselors can ask to get conversations started. Each table has a couple of super hero action figures on them. There is a raffle and a couple of skits. It's Awesome!
- Pizza Delivery - In the morning each cabin is given an order form. They get to choose up to 3 toppings for 3 pizzas and 3 activities. The pizzas are made and placed in a hot box to keep warm. Then they are delivered via golf cart to the cabins along with salad, 3 salad dressings, drinks, cookies, napkins, paper plates, plastic utensils, a garbage bag, and a box with their 3 chosen activities. The activity choices are a deck of cards, a specific board game, conversation starter pack, Simon Says, 20Q, Electronic Catch Phrase, Rubik's Cube, Story Cubes, etc. Afterward, the garbage and all the extras are picked up and returned to the kitchen by the activity staff.

DINNER
- Pirate Dinner - During this meal we decorate, wear pirate costumes and, because all the silverware went overboard, everyone must eat with kitchen utensils like spatulas, tongs, large wooden spoons, spaghetti servers, etc.
- Game Show Supper - We have different game shows each time we do this email. It could be a Let's Make a Deal, Minute To Win It, Deal or No Deal or something else. The main thing is that we give one camper per table a chance to play. If they win, the whole table gets a prize. The prize can be anything from a special dessert to camp store bucks to special privileges.

EXCLUSIVE CLUB

Our camp has a tradition of the "Order of the Fork." It's an exclusive club for campers and counselors who have particularly excellent table manners or mealtime habits (like drinking plenty of water or always finishing the salad).

During the week, every counselor nominates one camper from their table who deserves this award and gives them a fun name like "Laura Hydration-is-my-middle-name Smith." The directors also keep an eye on counselors and choose one to receive the award.

On our last day of the week, during lunch, there is a ceremony mid-mealtime. We have a HUGE carved fork and a long, silly speech describing a secret society that had a meeting the night before to decide upon the new members. They are then announced and brought to the front of the dining hall along with all pre-existing members to chant the secret code (please) getting louder and louder.

Finally the entire group makes a cha-cha type line and circles the dining hall singing "We are we are we are we are the order of the fork! (x2) And each and every one of us is sticking to the rest of us! We are we are we are we are the order of the fork!"

What other crazy (or serious) exclusive clubs could you come up with?

- The Carabiner Club (Ropes)
- The Snorkel Society (Waterfront)
- The Archers Alliance
- The Campfire Crew
- The Skit Syndicate
- The Lanyard Legion
- The Foto Federation (Photography)
- The Clean Cabin Coalition

FORMAL DINNERS

Most camps have some kind of a dress up or formal dinner for their Senior Teens Camp. We have taken it one more step and randomly make selections from our STAFF to couple together as a family to host a table for an elegant evening meal.

The campers are divided up to fill tables and participate willingly as they get to sit with and meet new people from outside of their normal friends group. One male and one female staff are chosen at random to be parents of this table and act accordingly for the meal time.

Where the twist and fun comes in is the PROPOSAL that needs to take place in order for the two staff to become a couple to host the family. It is all done in fun. During the earlier part of the week the male staff (alternates each year) must come up with a creative public proposal to ask the chosen female staff to be their date for the formal dinner. This has resulted in giant candle lit hearts with a piano serenade and a rented tux to "pop" the question.

Most of it is enhancing to the program and staff, but can cause undue pressure and shift the focus off the program if not carefully orchestrated.

———

At our camp we have a "formal" dinner. None of the campers actually wear anything special, but the staff try to dress up a bit in the spirit of the evening.

The staff are the "hoppers" - the ones to bring the food to the table. The main course, however, is brought out by the head cook/chef. He rolls out on a cart the meat, which he carves at the tables. One of the other cooks come out to help with another cart so campers aren't waiting all night to eat.

As soon as groups begin to finish their meal the chef brings out his cart again, this time with dessert. The dessert usually involves a kitchen torch in order to get the campers to go oooohh and aaaahh. The cooks love it. Sometimes, instead of pulling out the torch, the dessert cart has a choice of 4 or 5 desserts that each camper can choose as it goes by. The campers (and staff) are just as excited by that.

During the meal the staff are extra picky about table manners. They also give the campers some tips on table etiquette, which they learned during staff training.

Adding candles, cloth napkins and table cloths add to the atmosphere. One year we had a staff member who could play the violin. He played a bit for our special dinner. It was great.

ETIQUETTE DINNER

With our teen kids we do a fancy dinner on the last night of camp. The campers like to dress up (sometimes in costume, but usually they go for a snazzier look). Although the fancy dinner isn't so unusual, I think ours differs somewhat.

We make a point to teach our kids how to behave in these situations, how to dine out, how to use manners. It is essentially training as much as anything else. They are welcome to use it as a practice "date", but they have to behave like people old enough to date. The rules for arranging to sit with someone specific are: both people need to go to a Supervisor by lunch on the day of the dinner, unaided, and request that be seated together without giggles, tears, etc. If they can do that together, they can sit together. At our teen camp, there are many times throughout the week that relationships, respect, self worth are talked about and explored. The dinner is a chance to put these philosophies in action. They do remarkably well.

We begin the evening with some time to mingle and eat appetizers that are out on a serving table. We usually have live acoustic music playing and it gives the campers time to get there since the ladies always run late! It also gives them a chance to get the nervous giggles out and relax once they have debuted!

Once it's time to start officially, we have everyone go to their designated spot. Tables are set like you would find at a nice banquet facility. As far as the kitchen goes, they prepare a 4 or 5 course meal. It is served banquet style by the wait (program) staff. We usually have a soup course, a salad course, the main course, and then dessert.

Throughout the dinner, our Director gives tips like which utensil to use and why, what foods can be eaten with your fingers, how to place your silverware to indicate you are done eating, etc. The campers are reminded to practice having conversations that would be appropriate in mixed company. The wait staff is quite formal and the campers get a chance to practice asking for things politely from servers. Although we don't bill for the dinner, we go over what to expect and how to calculate a tip.

The kitchen works a little later than usual, but enjoys getting to prepare food in this way. We usually staff extra dishwashers, though, since we don't have enough plates otherwise. We've had to buy extra silverware, but everyone loves when they first walk in and sees the table settings. What to do with all that stuff?! Also, program staff needs to eat either before or after since they are busy bringing and clearing plates during the meal.

The whole event is really popular and I would like to point out at this camp, most of our kids are poor and many live in foster care. What we often hear is how it is not only the best meal they have ever had, but that the skills they learn are ones they go home and teach their own families and parents. I think that is soooo cool!

PART
5

EVENTS AND
CAMP WIDE GAMES

PIRATE'S GROG

A very special and magical ceremony we have is our annual Pirate's Grog. We celebrate the end of every week with a dress up themed Fiesta, and the Grog is the Fiesta ending our Pirate Week. We try to keep the actual Grog ceremony as simple as possible (as we've learned and attempted to do with most things), but it's just one of those magical events that, no matter our intentions, it just takes on a very HIGH SPIRITED life of its own once it begins.

We open the Grog ceremony with a little made up history of the Grog (we use the word Grog VERY loosely to mean motley pirate party).

Our Grog is a big ugly bowl of mixed dark sodas and juices. The making of the Grog is a big part of the ceremony. Each counselor brings a bottle of a drink re-labeled with names like Tarantula Venom, Black Tar Tonic, and Old Fish Snot, and one by one dumps their bottle into the Grog bowl with a short spooky story and lots of exaggerated drama.

Next, the Rules of the Mess are covered by the Pirate MC and everyone is told to never break the Rules of the Mess or risk getting sent to the Grog!

The rules are:
* Every sentence must start with "Argh!"
* Only use pirate names
* Sing at the top of your lungs, and call all your friends Me Hearties!

Immediately our pirates start breaking the rules and the counselors send them TO THE GROG. The campers love to get sent to the Grog! They fill their cup with the dark liquid, turn around to the whole crowd and say TO THE MESS, and the crowd shouts back WHAT A MESS! The pirate happily slurps down the liquid and returns to their seat to break the rules again! Pirate snacks (crackers and Swedish Fish) are served and gobbled.

Finally, the singing starts and sword fights break out everywhere. (Swords are loosely rolled up newspapers with duct tape - in fact, the whole week is called "Pirates Who Celebrate Duck Tape"). As camp ends for the day, the line for the Grog never gets shorter, and the day is talked about and relived the rest of summer.

LUAU AT THE POOL

The core of this activity is a pool party, but we add some things to spruce it up.

Smoothies
Grab a mix of fruit and other ingredients. Decide on three concoctions and give them some fancy names like Strawberry Sunset, Mango Magnific and Bodacious Berry. The kids really enjoy these treats.

Grilled fruit
We bring down a small grill and throw on some fruit (usually sliced pineapple) but you can do a few different fruits. If you really want to play it up, have staff walk around with serving trays of the fruit and drinks.

Lei making:
Teach the kids how to make flowers out of tissue paper, and let them make leis. There are several different ways to make tissue-paper flowers- you can find a lot online.

Music:
Music always makes an activity that much better. If you can find some luau music to mix in, it makes the theme stronger. But be sure to play some hits, too!

Photos:
Anytime you have an event that will be remembered by the campers and staff, make sure you take a lot of photos that you can add to an end of session slideshow.

Attire:
Staff (and campers) pull out the Hawaiian Shirts, Hawaiian dresses, and hula skirts.

A NIGHT AT THE OSCARS

We go all out for this event to make it unforgettable!

- Staff dress up as celebs, while others provide security detail.
- We have a red carpet event complete with interviews, cameras flashing, and autographs.
- Inside the Oscars venue we decorate with movie posters that we have been collecting for eons plus other film-related paraphernalia.
- We provide "movie" snacks -- popcorn, Junior Mints or Snowcaps, and a special Oscar statue cookie (check out pinterest -- you'll find one).
- As groups enter, they are assigned a celeb (counselor) with whom to sit and who will serve as a team leader.
- The actual event involves watching clips from movies and answering trivia questions (as a team) about obscure items from the clips. We might do 6 to 10 clips depending on length of clips and interest -- so we show the clip, then ask a series of questions (3 to 5 depending on clip), then move on to the next clip. We're not big on the competition part because our kids just love the event but we do review the answers for those who must know.
- We, of course, have "entertainment" as well as commercials during the event.
- We have also included camper-produced film debuts at this event.
- We're thinking of creating an after-Oscars party for older groups.

WALK THE PLANK

Last year we tried out an interesting new idea for an evening event. Generally our evening events are held in our dining hall, our amphitheater where we have our campfires or in our big sandy/ dirt parking lot. We decided to try out a full camp event at the pool for a change. Our theme for the day was "Under the Sea" and we were doing color wars for the week, so we created a game called "Walk the Plank: Pirate Trivia" with the camp broken into its 4 teams.

We had all the campers and counselors sitting in their teams at the shallow end of the pool. We had a projector and Jeopardy style PowerPoint on with our sound system and the host for the evening, a real live pirate! (All electrical was covered and well out of the splash zone)

At the deep end of the pool we set up 4 planks leading into the water. Each team selected one of their counselors to "walk the plank" and act as a game piece. The game plays round robin (buzzers would be preferred, but were too complicated for the pool). Get the question right, and your game piece steps backwards towards safety. Get the question wrong and you step forward toward the shark-infested pool. too many wrong answers and your player "walks the plank" (as the entire camp cheers their demise) and that team is out of the round. Last team standing wins the round (or first team to back off the plank with correct answers wins)

But wait, there's more! The questions get more difficult as you progress through each topic (our topics ranged from Pirates, shark knowledge, sea life, local sports team trivia, camp history, etc). Scoring was based on the round instead of by the question (made things a lot easier) and the kids were competing for our host's treasure chest full of color war points.

Instead of a daily double, we interspersed the game with "physical challenge" games, similar to "Double Dare". Each team would select 2 participants to compete in the physical challenge. A few of our challenges were "splash attack" where one wears goggles and holds a cup on a stick in their mouth while player 2 splashes them in the face. Player 1 tries to be the first to collect water up to the line on the cup. One other challenge was "David Hasselhoff's Muscle Beach Flex-off" where participants (preferably a group of overzealous scrawny 6 year olds) were selected by their team to flex their best muscle pose and be judged by a panel of non biased nurses. It was absolutely hilarious.

We wrapped up a few rounds of walk the plank trivia with a full-camp night-swim. Note, there are many considerations to take into account before attempting a full camp event at the pool: camp size, pool size, lifeguards, insurance, area capacity, and medical considerations, just to name a few. For our camp, it worked well. The trivia game and night swim were a success (as well as a learning experience) and everyone had a great time.

HAUNTED HOUSE

Once a summer (because it's quite a bit of work to pull off) we set up an optional haunted house for teen campers.

We have decor specifically for this event, Halloween items we've gotten on sale through the years such as hanging skeletons, masks, and a fog machine.

We set up probably 8 'stations' around camp, and campers go on a hike/tour that walks through all 8. A staff member or two are at each station, pretending to be dead, being a ghost, with a scary mask on, popping out and scaring people, etc.

A tour guide goes with each group and tells the tale/story of "The haunted…at Camp _____" whatever!

To make it scarier, make details have to do with your specific camp or camp locations. We warn them ahead of time that this is an optional activity, and if they're going to be too scared and stay up all night, they need to make a responsible choice (to not do the haunted house) and go play cards or have an alternate program!

It really is quite a hit, and something they definitely remember.

PIRATE HUNT

At my camp, once a summer we have a pirate hunt which is one of the campers' favorite things of the summer. Here is what we do..

- The whole camp comes together, and are split into groups of 8-10, and one staff member is assigned to this group.
- Meanwhile, the rest of the staff are dressed as pirates, and are given an area to hide in camp.
- The pirates hide a sword near where they are hiding, then they themselves hide.
- The children have 80 minutes to find as many pirates as they can.
- When the children find the pirates, they have to bring them down to jail (we use the swimming changing rooms), and this is decorated with pirate flags on the inside and signs such as 'Pirates ye be warned'.
- The pirates can try and escape jail, and the staff usually do this when the children are close so that the children get the fun of stealing them again!
- There is also a treasure chest hidden somewhere around camp, and if this is found it has to be given to a staff member who is guarding the jail.
- After the 80 minutes is up, the bell rings and everyone goes down to the beach by the lake.
- After all the children are back, the pirates are then brought from jail by the 2 guards. The guards then take them out and throw then into the lake, but only if their sword was found. Pirates who were not found are not thrown into the lake.
- The treasure is always found, as it is usually hidden somewhere noticeable, and all the children get a reward from what is inside, usually something small like a pirate tattoo, and the group that found it gets an eye patch, or something pirate-ish like this. It is always really fun, and the kids love seeing their favorite staff members thrown into the lake.

STAFF

- There is 1 staff member per group. The number of groups depends on amount of children. You don't want groups that are huge, otherwise not all children will have a part to play in the capturing.
- There are 2 guards at the jail.
- All other staff members are pirates (more pirates the better).

PROPS

- 1 map per group - this shows boundaries where pirates are hiding. this is usually stained with tea and has burn marks on it, just to make it look old.
- Pirate flags
- Signs for decorating treasure chest (can be made from old cardboard box)
- Small prizes (e.g. tattoos, eye patches)
- Enough pirate swords for all pirates with staff members name on them (need to know what pirates have been found)

GLOW IN THE DARK CAPTURE THE FLAG

One of my favorite evening activities would have to be glow in the dark capture the flag. The standard rules of capture the flag are used but teams set out to hide their "flag" or other object in the dark of the woods somewhere.

Have campers during the day create their team "idol" for hiding in the woods. We used stuffed animals that were taped to sticks which worked well. "Flags" had to be surrounded by glow sticks so that they were at least visible for the teams when searching for them.

Flashlights are recommended as walking around in the woods can be difficult at night and glow sticks add another cool dimension to the game. Prisoners must freeze where they are when tagged, until they are found and released by another team mate. (Honor system must come into play here.... and yes people will cheat.)

This is best done at camps where there are established trails to follow. You will want to be sure to establish clear boundaries with the campers about how much you will allow them to leave the trail. For example, do they have to stay directly on the trail, can they venture into the woods for 5-10 feet to avoid being "captured", etc.

It is extremely important if you choose to play this that you have some type of bullhorn, camp wide PA system or other way of calling campers back in when the game is over.

There's also a new system that uses LED lights specifically designed for Capture the Flag games in the dark. It's called Capture the Flag Redux. Whole this system will cost more than just buying glow sticks, most of it runs on batteries making a better environmental choice.

STALK THE LANTERN

Our favorite evening activity is called Stalk the Lantern...it originates from South Africa and we put a few variations on it to make it safe for camp!

We use it as one of our color competition events, but it can easily be changed to be a cabin activity too. It is played on a dark night- preferably no moon!

- There is a center 'lantern' that is made up of 3 people (either the directors or senior staff members). Each of these people has a flashlight.
- The staff are in concentric circles going out from the lantern...and are assigned point values. The lantern is worth 100 points, the next circle 20, the next 10, the next 5 etc. You can make the points whatever number you wish, and as many circles as you like too. Just ensure that the staff are not too spread out, as they provide the supervision to the game.
- The campers are assigned starting points outside the last staff circle and have to crawl or creep as quietly as possible and try to 'stalk' the lantern.
- The people in the middle with the flashlights try to spot the campers as they crawl. If they see movement or hear noise they shine their flashlight (briefly) and if it is a camper they are instructed to go to the nearest counselor in front of them.
- The point value is written on the camper's hand, and they then go to a specified building to record their points and to sit quietly until the game is over.
- The campers wear black, and there are safety rules that we have for our own camp. Each camp will have to make their own set of rules, applicable to their facilities.
- The last circle, before reaching the lantern, is worth 50 points. The campers have to actually touch the lantern in order to score 100.

It is extremely popular among our kids!!! They get completely into it!! We also announce it in fun, surprise ways and pretend it is far later than it actually is! Also, we only play for 15 minutes, although the campers will all tell you it is at least an hour! It is such a lot of fun and every camp should play it!!! All the counselors should have flashlights and washable markers...and it is a good idea to check comfortable places for campers who have fallen asleep. We had an 8-year old sleeping in a tube!!

INTERNATIONAL EVENT

About 30% of our staff is international and we ask them to bring songs, games, stories, etc. from their home country. We used to focus on one country or region each session, but now we do more of a bazaar, showcasing all countries each week.

Ideas from past years:
- USA football and a wagon ride
- Irish dancing
- PowerPoint Presentations
- Songs
- Rugby and other popular games
- Candies or other treats

We usually have 2-3 time blocks and the kids can choose where they want to go. We start and end all together and may have national anthems, a skit or other fun activities.

We also have a special all camp dinner outside (instead of in the dining hall) and usually do something like Mexican or Chinese (with chopsticks).

International campers also help plan activities if they wish.

HUMANS vs. ZOMBIES

An Evening Activity Created By Scott Chernoff, Counselor, and the Campers from Roaring Brook Camp for Boys, Inc.

- Set boundaries with the group as needed for safety and communication.
- Everybody has a headlamp/flashlight.
  - HUMANS always have their light on
  - ZOMBIES always have their light off
- Begin with 3 ZOMBIES. Choose 3 kids (Be creative in the selection such as 3 from New Jersey, redheads, skateboard shoes, etc.). Have them demonstrate their best ZOMBIE stumble/walk prior to the start of the game.
- Everyone else is a HUMAN.
- To turn a HUMAN into a ZOMBIE, a ZOMBIE must tap a HUMAN on top of the head. The ZOMBIFIED victim must then turn their headlight/flashlight off and proceed to stumble/walk like a ZOMBIE to pursue the rest of the HUMANS.
- The game ends when everyone becomes a ZOMBIE or when one HUMAN survives the "Attack of the ZOMBIES".

Variations:

1. Survival:
   - The HUMANS are released. The ZOMBIES are released 10 seconds later.
   - A timer begins allowing 10 minutes from when the ZOMBIES are released with a loud signal device (a loud gong, symbol crash, etc.).
   - The object is to survive 10 minutes without becoming a ZOMBIE.
   - At the end of 10 minutes make a loud signal.
   - All the survivors are winners.
2. Mission:
   - Hide a flag in the forest prior to the game start.
   - Release the HUMANS first, and then 5 ZOMBIES are released 5 seconds later with a loud signal.
   - Object: Humans must find the flag. The winner is the HUMAN who returns with the flag.
   - ZOMBIES must stay 50 feet (well away) from the "hidden" flag until a HUMAN attempts to carry it back to the start.
   - The head-tap rule doesn't apply in this version. ZOMBIES only need to tag HUMAN with the flag to ZOMBIFY them. When ZOMBIFICATION occurs, the former HUMAN must drop the flag and move as quickly as a ZOMBY can stumble away from the dropped flag until another HUMAN attempts to make a "run for it" to take the flag back to the start area.

CAMPER SNEAK

We do this with our youngest campers only. They seem to get into it the most.

A letter is placed in each cabin while the campers are out doing an activity. Kids love surprises. When the campers return to their cabin for the night, they read the letter which tells them that there is some TOP SECRET information which they are to share with no one.

They get to sneak out of their cabin at exactly "9:51 pm" (times are staggered between cabins). They are told they need to sneak as quietly as possible without being seen, to a specified location.

Once they arrive, there is a special treat (s'mores or whatever).

The letter also says that they are NOT to tell the boys (or girls). We have our boys cabins and girls cabins sneak on the same night but to different sides of the camp.

Counselors are instructed to help them "sneak" with as much stealth as possible. It's super cute to see campers running from behind a tree...to behind a garbage can for fear of being seen.

GLOW IN THE DARK EGG HUNT

Glow in the Dark Easter Egg Hunt (Can be played in teams or individually)

- Buy plastic Easter Eggs (best time to stock up is after Easter when they are on sale)
- Cut little strips of paper and write a number of each one (need 1 piece per egg). The numbers can range from 1-? anywhere really or you could use 0 but we prefer not to. Number can be used more than once!!!
- Put a piece of paper in each egg
- This next step will vary...A-buy glow in the dark egg (found this image on google so you have an idea) or B-get regular eggs and but glow sticks to put inside them
- Have someone (or several people) hide the eggs. Then let the campers go find them. (we use Wal-Mart bags to collect eggs)
- A variation would be to do some sort of relay for each team and have part of the relay be to grab an egg
- Once everyone has an egg or they are all found (would recommend a count before hiding them and after finding them) have the groups/individual open their eggs and add up the total number of points inside all the eggs
- Winner has the most points and you can award a prize...we do a small prize for everyone and a bigger prize for the winner

The catch is that having the most eggs does not guarantee that you will win.

LETTER TO MYSELF

Each session we have campers write themselves a letter about the week, what they learned, new friends, hopes for the future, etc. They turn in the letter to us and it is sent to them at Christmas.

This is a great way to continue the camp spirit at a low time of the year. It also gets them ready to register for next year!

What makes this so memorable is not only that we send them out during the winter but it's how we set-up our lodge and make it, more-or-less, event-like.

The photo below is our lodge at night while the letter writing is going on.

As you can see using a lot of candles sets a wonderful mood, especially in a lodge like this. Provide the campers with paper, envelopes and pens. When they are finished they can give their envelopes to a staff member and then go into another room to socialize or participate in an activity. The place they are writing their letters should be quiet - no talking.

Want to make this extra special? Make sure the campers do not seal the envelopes. Let them know that a special "something" will be added to the envelope. They cannot know what it is until they get it in the mail in December. What can you add? Here are a couple of suggestions - a letter from their counselor, camp store bucks to be used when they return, a group photo, fun shaped confetti, a camp sticker, or a special award certificate.

CELEBRATING HP

Harry Potter's birthday is July 31 so we celebrate this with trips to:

Honeydukes
At this candy shop kids get to make their own candy, decorate cupcakes, make ice cream, and/ or bake cookies.

Olivander's Wand Shop
Here the kids get to make their own wands using chopsticks, markers, ribbon, beads, glitter and cord.

Slug and Jiggers Apothecary
The kids get all their potion ingredients and instructions from this shop. They then use them to create potions (science experiments). We get a lot of ideas from Steve Spangler's website.

Eeylops Owl Emporium
Unfortunately, right before the kids get here the owls had escaped. It is up to the kids to find them. There are three owls (stuffed animals) hidden in the area.

Weasley's Wizard Wheezes
It's our lucky day, because today they have a magician performing here. Sometimes we have someone on staff that can do magic tricks, and other times we have to find a parent or even hire a magician to come in.

The Leaky Cauldron
Finally, the kids get to relax and have a cup of Butterbeer. Some kids like it and others don't so we have other drinks available with crazy names.

When the kids hear we are having a Harry Potter celebration some of them come in with cloaks and wand and lightning bolt scars on their foreheads.

We'll also divide the kids into houses and have a Harry Potter trivia contest. This day is always a favorite of camp.

FULL MOON MADNESS

Full Moon Madness occurs whenever there is a Full Moon. Since that only happens once a month it is a very special occasion, and therefore, very memorable. We even have campers who know about this event look up the dates of the full moons and register for those weeks.

It all starts with a staff member running into the dining hall the morning of a full moon. He is ina panic and announces that tonight they should lock themselves in their cabins, because tonight is the night he turns into a werewolf. Then another staff member stands up and says, "Instead of locking ourselves up tonight, we'll just lock you up.

That's when the song Thriller begins. All the campers cheer because they know that tonight will be the Full Moon Madness.

Activities we have done in the past include:
- Glow Stick Capture the Flag
- Night Hikes
- Pool Parties
- Carnivals
- Dances
- Nighttime Dodgeball
- Kitchen Raids
- Crazy campfires
- S'more bar
- Night sailing
- Scavenger Hunts
- Flashlight Tag
- Game Shows

What makes this night so special is that activities run until midnight. The older kids have hunts and challenges even after that. The next morning breakfast is an hour later and everyone comes in their PJs. There is a bed head contest, a best of pajamas contest, and cartoons are played through a projector onto the wall.

Half way through breakfast the staff person who turned into a werewolf is let out of the locked room. His shirt is torn up and there is extra hair on his face as though he had just turned back. Then someone yells, "We all survived!" and everyone cheers again.

It's an epic night that we try to top every month.

A MEMORABLE CAPTURE THE FLAG VARIATION

This game is a variation on Capture the flag that evolved from years of seeing problems with the game. Capture the Flag is a truly great game that can inspire stories that last a life time. We set out to improve it. Our version is called SAVE THE WHALES!

Like Capture the Flag, Save the Whales can be played on a large open field, but is better over a larger area with varied terrain and obstacles. Unlike, Capture the Flag there is no need to establish a mid-line and there is no need for a jail. Both of these features in Capture the Flag encouraged cheating or unsportsmanlike teasing rather than actual playing by the rules. Just set the outer boundaries and send one team to one end and the other to the other end.

The use of two differently colored, blow-up whales instead of flags and the subsequent name change was because the Mennonite camp that I worked at didn't like Capture the Flag because it was a war simulation game. The use of whales also enhanced the pictures from the game as well.

Each team is given a whale and flag football flags equal to 1.5 times the number of players per team (50 players on a team = 50 belts and 75 flags of the same color to each team). Obviously the two teams need different colors (Now that I think about it, this might play just as well with 3 or 4 teams provided that they each had their own color of flags).

Each team is also appointed a team captain, el Presidente, a mature counselor who manages organization, strategy, rule enforcement and distribution of the team flags. El Presidente does not need a belt or personal flag because (s)he stays with the whale the whole time and cannot be "killed".

The objective of the game is simple: get the other team's whale and return it to your President. You can only be "in-play" if you are wearing a personal flag. If your flag is taken, you must return to your president or another teammate who is carrying a spare flag to get back "in-play".

I used to tell a story of two oceanic research groups who had divergent theories as to how to save the whales. I made the story fairly elaborate, but the gist was that there were only two known whales in captivity and that they had to be together in order to reproduce and neither side was willing to share their whale with the other group and so the lead Biologist from each group had determined that taking the other group's whale was the only solution.

After the story is told and the rules explained, each team is given about 15 minutes to get to their end of the game zone, distribute their belts and flags, throw together a strategy, and place their whale. El Presidente, will need to use this time wisely and be completely familiar with the rules. For example the whales must be placed in an open visible area (the game is not called Hide the Whale for a reason), and once it is placed neither he nor any other of his team can move it. He can provide instruction and give guidance but el Presidente stays with the whale. If the other team moves the whale he must stay with it.

After the personal flags are distributed there will be extra flags that the president has to hold onto. A prearranged signal will mark the beginning of actual play, no offensive operations are to begin before the signal.

When play begins everyone with a flag is active, "in-play". If a player takes a flag from another player, the person becomes inactive but the flag remains active until it is given to el Presidente. For example, Yellow-man A gets in a showdown with Red-man A and Yellow-man ends up with a red flag in his hand (Be sure to explain that there is no intentional contact allowed to get a flag and there is no hiding or holding your own flag to keep it from being taken). Red-man A must immediately drop anything he has and begin returning to his president for another red flag. Yellow-man A can take the red flag to Yellow President to have it taken out of the game, or pass it to Yellow-man B to take back.

If a player has his personal flag taken while carrying other flags, he must surrender the carried flags to the one who took his flag. In this way a person can actually end-up with both colors of active flags. A carrier can serve as a "medic" and provide a teammate with an appropriate colored flag (but not his own flag). This flag system eliminates the need for a jail. Motivated players will rush back and get another flag, while unmotivated players will mosey back.

Eventually, attrition begins to take effect as flags are taken out of play. Before long even the defenders close to the whale may not find it possible to get a new flag and return to their posts.

When an active player from an opposing team grabs the whale the game is not yet over. The whale must make it back to the other president. The same rules apply for carrying the whale as carrying extra flags. It can be passed to other active teammates, but if the carrier's flag is taken the whale must be left in place. However, unlike a surrendered flag, a dropped whale does not get to go back to its original location. It must be guarded where it falls.

Obviously, many of my terms and explanations of the rules reflect the evolution from the war simulation game, Capture the Flag. However, they are unimportant. Change the item that is carried and sync up the terminology with the story that you are telling for that week and you have a game that enhances your theme and will become an instant classic.

CHAOS VS. CONTROL

The campers play as their color war teams (but dress all in one color so that the teams are not obvious) and the counselors dress in black. It is team vs. team; counselors vs. kids and kids vs. counselors.

There are 3 ticketing stations. The campers need a ticket to play, which they collect from an assigned station. The other stations increase the ticket value if the camper can get there without being tagged by a counselor. If the camper is tagged they have to hand their ticket to the counselor and return with hands in the air to the assigned first station.

The counselors are wearing flag football belts (you can also use socks). If the camper can grab a belt and return it to their 'safe zone' they receive 50 points. They need to return without being tagged by another counselor. If a counselor has lost their belt they cannot tag campers until they get their belt back (if the belt is turned in for points the counselor can go and retrieve their belt!). The counselors try to collect as many tickets from the kids as possible.

There is also a hidden item (we use a bugle). No-one know where this is! If a camper finds it and returns it to the safe zone they get 100 points! The counselors may not search for the bugle but will want to try to tag the campers if they get it to avoid them getting points.

In the safe zone there are 3 collection points - one for each camper team and one for the counselors. The campers can turn in their tickets at any time - no matter how many stations they have been to safely. Each station is an additional point (we use a hole puncher to add the points - no holes is 1 point, 1 hole is 3 points and 2 holes is 5 points). When the counselors have too many tickets they return them here too.

At the end we add up all the points - there is a winning color war team and a winner between campers and counselors. If the campers beat the counselors we have the counselors do cabin clean-up the next day, or waitress the next day (something small and fun for the kids).

You have to have assigned boundaries - no inside buildings, no lakefront etc. Also, each ticketing zone should have cones around to mark it and if a kid gets within the cones they are safe. Counselors who are unable to run can man these areas.

This is an all-time favorite among campers and counselors- and a great way to wear the camp out before bedtime!!

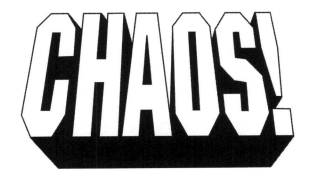

HUMAN CLUE

The camp is divided into smaller groups which must gather clues from staff members, dressed and acting as Clue characters, scattered throughout the site. It's a process of elimination type game, where at the end it is revealed who was the murderer, where it took place, and with what weapon. Of course the "murderer" is thrown into the lake as a punishment for his/her crimes!

Materials
Enough clue sheets for each team (listing all the possibilities for WHO, WHERE, WITH WHAT -- the more possibilities the longer the game. I usually stick with about 15 clues total for an 1.5 hour game on a fairly big/spread out site. Not all the Clue characters have to be suspects), a pen/pencil for each team, costumes for the staff (dressing up as Colonel Mustard, Mr, Green, etc, but also you can add some of your own like Mrs. Green, the wife of Mr. Green or Miss Violet, Scarlet's best friend, etc).

Before the game
Take a clue sheet and cut it so you have slips of paper with a single clue on it. Take one WHO, one WHERE, and one WITH WHAT and put it somewhere secret (I like putting it in my sock!)... this is the ANSWER. Distribute the remaining clues to the staff members who are suspects & additional characters. These are the clues they will eventually give to the campers.

Game Flow
Usually, I'll start by announcing dramatically that there has been a death and that we need to figure it out. It's often more fun if I frame it as if I am a detective investigating the murder and I need the kids help to solve the crime swiftly.

I will introduce the possible suspects of the crime - and all the staff members in character. I let the staff scatter and then explain to the campers that I bet the suspects know more than they let on. I need them to find them to get more information.

I then split them into groups (usually mixed ages, having the older campers/LITs in charge of ensuring the group stays together since you can't get a clue unless the whole team is there) and explain the Clue Sheets before sending them off.

Essentially, they will approach a character and ask for a clue. They will need to complete a task designated by the character first. Once completed, the staff member will give them a clue (the one you gave them before the game started) to scratch off their list. Essentially, they are getting clues as to what did NOT happen. I explain they they will eventually be left with only one WHO, one WHERE and one WITH WHAT clue left on their sheet - this is the answer!

Once they have gathered what they believe to be the solution they must return to a designated place (campfire pit, the docks, etc... where ever your camp's meeting place is). Once everyone has arrived, the staff/characters also return. A dramatic unfolding of the murder case occurs. I love when the staff get really into it and act out what happened and improv their motives for the crime. As the detective in charge of the case, I will usually call for justice and take suggestions from the campers on how to deal with the murderer... almost always it's a dunk in the lake and justice is served

There are many alternative ways of playing this game. One way is to have stations that the groups rotate through (visiting a new character at each rotation) as opposed to a more free-for-all run around trying to find staff. This makes it less of a race and competition but may require a bit more organization about how rotations happen (how often and where to go next, etc).

Also, for another variation, you could theme it any way you would like. Are you having a magic theme day? Have the staff dress as wizard/witches/magical creatures and change the weapons to things like magic wands and magician hats).

Is there a winning group? If so, how is that determined?
*Note: I don't always do a winning group, although I have in the past. When I do, the winning group is the first group back to me with with what they feel to be the correct answer. If they are the first group back, I'll put a #1 on their clue sheet and then a #2 to the next group and so on. But I don't usually come back to it, because my experience is that the revelation of the solution is pretty exciting and the kids forget about who was done first and just want to know if they got their answer right!

Clue

MUD DAY EVENT

Campers wear old t-shirts and shorts or bathing suits and participate in various activities with the focus on getting dirty!

There is a mud pit station, a slip and slide station (water only for safety reasons), mud body painting, mud play dough sculpting, mud facials and foot soak. Groups rotate through the different stations and then to wrap up the event our local fire truck brings one of their water pumper trucks and we all shower off under the spray from the fire truck. The kids and the volunteer fire fighters just love this ending.

We run this event for approximately 2 hours for campers age 5-10 years. For us the most important part is the early and regular communication with parents so they know what to expect from a clothing stand point.

Needed for the event:
* An open space where it is ok to create a mud puddle
* Clean mud (no stone/rock chunks) soil works great
* Slip and slide
* Water from outside tap
* Paint brushes, trays
* Play dough recipe: ½ cup of cold water, 1 tablespoon cooking oil, 2 tablespoons brown tempera paint, ½ cup of salt, 1 tablespoon cornstarch and 1 ½ cups of white flour
* Road access or a parking lot close by to meet the fire truck
* A camera to record all the great faces and fun

There is actually an international mud day and here is the website: www.worldforumfoundation.org/working-groups/nature/international-mud-day/

TAKESHI'S CHALLENGE

This event needs to be run in stages, like a massive obstacle course all over camp. Try keeping them all in view of the others so that they can all have a good laugh at the other teams.

Each obstacle needs to be competed by all of the kids in the team. The things they need to do at each station need to be completely theme related and completely absurd:

- Have the whole team try to score 10 goals in the basketball hoops while wearing a snorkeling mask.
- Kids need to complete a race where EVERY person in the team is tied together at the ankles.
- Have croquet set up and have the team try to complete it while having their hands tied behind their backs.
- Teams need to make it across the pool on pool noodles, underwater skateboards, dolphins, etc. (Make sure that you have a lifeguard stationed at the pool.)
- Human Foosball – (here you will need 2 teams going up against each other) In the hall mark out 3 rows for each team. Have a couple of kids on each line trying to score goals. They can only move up and down their row.
- Fill a box/a few different crates with colored balls and have a random object somewhere in one of the crates for the kids to find using their faces (marble, ping pong ball etc.).

These are just some of the things that I like to see. The teams get throughout he stations pretty quickly. It's best if you have more stations than you have groups. Any team can go to any station that is empty. You can either have counselors at the stations while each group is assigned a leader or a CIT leads them around, or you can have the counselors lead their group to the different stations and also be the one to explain the rules - essentially make the stations unmanned.

EVERY CHILD needs to be involved AS part of the TEAM and needs to have a chance at EVERY station!!!!! This means you'll need to create stations that all kids will be okay with. If you have an overweight camper, or a camper with a scar on his back who doesn't want to take off their shirt to go into the pool, have a challenge where a couple of the teammates need to help outside of the pool. Don't have super athletic games that a non athletic camper will never be able to accomplish. Things like that.

Takeshi's Challenge is the name of a horribly reviewed Nintendo video game from 1980s. I don't know why this camp event is called Takeshi's Challenge. I'm thinking that it's because the video game is absurd. But don't worry, this even t is MUCH more fun than the video game!

STAFF vs. STAFF PLAY-OFF

Every Friday, we divide the staff into teams, mixing some of the older kids to join in (or anyone that really wanted to play).

Games can be anything (football, basketball, dodgeball, quidditch, ultimate Frisbee, a triva contest, etc.). The event lasts around an hour and a half.

We have all of the kids choose their favorite team, that way the staff had their own cheer team on the side line cheering them on. We had the kids make signs for their team and gave them their own team names; some of the kids give nicknames to staff members also.

During half time (45 min into the first half of the game) we throw rolled up t-shirts, toys and big candy bars to the kids in the stands. The kids thought it was great.

We started out just planning on doing this once for the camp, but it became one the most requested activity during the whole summer camp. Staff enjoyed it, and seeing the kids really get into it was fabulous!

CHRISTMAS IN JULY

This is an activity we did with our 5-6 year olds. We realized/remembered how much we loved Christmas as little kids so we made Christmas in the summer.

- We got fake snow and put it all over a room we were using
- Found decorations in the storage room and put up a tree
- Had the kids decorate the tree when they came into the room
- Had hot chocolate and Christmas music playing
- Played Christmas versions of camp games

There are many other things you can do besides the above, including:

- Having snowball fights using "Snowtime Anytime" from Amazon.com
- Hire a Santa to visit or rent a Santa costume to use
- Bake Christmas cookies
- Hold a gift exchange
- Make paper snowflakes
- Have a turkey feast for dinner
- Place cinnamon-apple scented pinecones in the rooms
- Make gingerbread houses
- Wrap doors like presents
- Have staff dress as elves
- Hire someone to bring in a snow-making machine
- Rent a fake ice skating rink
- Watch a Christmas movie like Elf or A Christmas Story
- Interject Christmas traditions from other countries

FOOD NETWORK COMPETITION DAY

The "biggest hit" of our previous summer was the Food Network Competition Day. Our kids love anything involving food.

Here are the activities that we did that particular day:

FOOD CATEGORY GAME
Our group was divided into three teams. Each team was given a food category such as "meat," "dairy" or "fruit and vegetable." I wrote the names of foods belonging to these food groups on paper plates and taped them to the gym wall. One person at a time went up to the wall and found an item in their food group, pulled it down and took it back to the group. The first group with all 20 was the winner. We had older kids help the younger ones in this game.

FRUIT BY THE FOOT COMPETITION
I cut strips of "Fruit by the Foot" in half and used clothes pins to attach them to string about 10 foot long. The strips were about 6" apart. I had enough for each child already set up. Staff held the ends of the strings and the kids raced two at a time to eat the hanging fruit leather from the bottom to the clothespin without using their hands.

CHEESE BALL EATING CONTEST
I put Cheetos cheese balls on paper plates and the kids came up in small groups to race and eat the cheese balls with no hands.

M&M CANDY GAME
I had two teams of 6 on each side of a 6 foot table racing for this game. I had sheets of colored paper in the colors of the M&M's in front of each pair of kids facing each other. I started with two small bowls of candy at one end of the table. The first pair found all the candy in their color in their bowls and ate them, then passed the bowl to the next person on their team who would find all the candy in their assigned color and then pass it on. First team with an empty bowl won.

CHEEZ-IT WORD FIND
I found some Cheez-It with letters printed on them. I gave 3 teams of older kids each a box and they had to make as many words within time limit as possible.

FOOD DICE GAME
I found 6 interesting looking foods and gave them creative names. I labeled the food items 1 to 6. Kids rolled a dice to see which item they tried.

BABY FOOD ROULETTE
I placed baby food jars around the edge of a lazy susan. Kids took turns spinning to see what they got to try.

PART 6

ONGOING COMPETITIONS AND CHALLENGES

CAMP CHALLENGES

Camp challenges are always memorable at camp. We still have kids years later talking about them. So, to avoid the "I'm bored" statement, we offer camp challenges. A poster is displayed with about 10 challenges that can be done at camp during "down time".

Some examples are:

- Write a poem about what camp means to you.
- Make a friendship bracelet for someone in your group.
- Come up with a cabin rap.
- Build a raft that will float a stuffed animal.
- Make a center piece using only items found in nature.
- Build a fairy house.
- Make a welcome sign in front of your cabin with rocks.
- Find the 10 secret items hidden around camp.
- Do something nice for someone at camp.
- Create a decoration piece for your cabin based on the theme of the week.

The list can be endless. Different ones are created for every camp and try to have them match the theme of camp.

After they complete each challenge they receive a ribbon, laminated shape, icon or bead of some kind. Again, it usually matches the theme. They collect all 10 on a safety pin to put on their camp hat as a memory. These are always optional and the kids love collecting all 10 goodies. We have also had bingo chips where they get so many chips per challenge. At the end of camp they spend their chips on prizes we offer.

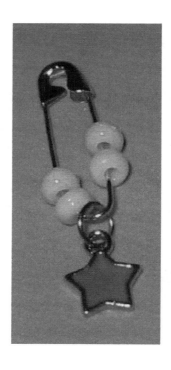

SUMMER LONG CAPTURE THE FLAG

Each year there is a camp-wide game of capture the flag that occurs ALL SUMMER LONG. This is not your ordinary game of Capture the Flag, however.

Every unit leader creates a flag and must carry it with them as they travel around camp. They can either have the kids carry it or one of the other unit staff members can carry it. If the unit should happen to leave or forget the flag somewhere, it can be "rescued" by another staff member or unit.

In order for the unit to get their flag back they must spin the "Wheel of Consequences". There are a variety of consequences including:
- The whole unit must do a dance number in front of the camp.
- The unit leader gets pied in the face.
- All counselors of the unit must serve the food dishes to all tables at the next meal.
- All campers and staff of the unit eat last for the next 3 meals

These are just examples. There are more and they change constantly. Also, on the prize wheel there is alway one good consequence as well. For example, "The unit gets to eat first for the next 3 meals".

BOOK OF RECORDS

We started a book of records for our summer program. This is a specific event where campers can invent their own challenge or try to break the record of an existing one.

There is no limit to the amount of times they can try during the event of the number of records they can try to beat (or set).

We have a record keeper, time keeper and photographer. Some of the past challenges have been:
- The most trash collected
- The longest consecutive time jump roping
- Farthest football throw
- Longest time spent doing the cup game

Campers came up with some crazy things for a record. As long as it was safe and appropriate, it was allowed.

Another variation from a different camp...

BOOK OF RECORDS II
Around our main area of camp we set up many stations with different types of challenges. The campers can roam free and choose any challenge that they want. Each station keeps track of the winners (older boy, older girl, younger boy, younger girl, and counselor) and at the end of the night, we all go back into the dining hall for the awards ceremony.

Some stations last summer included:
- Chugging water (promotes hydration)
- Wheelbarrow race
- Planking
- One girl chose to stand on one foot for the entire 60 minutes
- Saying the alphabet backwards

The great thing about this program is that you can have many different types of challenges and allow the campers to choose whatever they want to do.

GAME SHOW WEEK

Game Shows?!? What could be more fun? There are a gazillion game shows out there that can be incorporated into every activity at camp. Some of the Game Shows will last for one meal and others for the whole week!

ARRIVAL
Cash Cab Counselors
The counselors that are taking in the kids bags will at random play Cash Cab while carrying the kids bags, the kids having to answer a question for every 2m or so. (drop offs only)

Mystery Cabin Counselor
After counselors have introduced themselves one from each cabin will go up to their cabin and hide somewhere. The cabins will be split up without that counselors name being mentioned. The kids will guess which is their counselor and will only find out once they get to their cabin.

Cabin shuffle
Kids won't be told the name of their cabin but will have to guess from a series of clues from their counselors. When they get it right they'll go up and find their Mystery Counselor.

ALL WEEK
Counselors will be allocated a Game that they are in charge of for the week.

What are the prizes? Counselors will be given tasks that they have to do for the campers. Some will include making the kids bed, carrying their bag, piggy back rides, designated high-fiver, body guard, clearing their dishes, etc. We call prizes "Oompa Loompas".

Cash Cab
A different counselor will be appointed Cash Counselor every time groups go up to the cabins. The counselor will stop their cabin along the board-walk and offer them a reward in exchange for the right answers to the 5-10 questions. The rewards will be things that the counselors will do for them (Oompa Loompas), so each kid can get a different reward for a right question.

Counselor Swap
Every siesta cabins will trade a counselor with another cabin (like the show Wife Swap) and they'll get a feel for different counselors.

Host Announcements
Every announcement during the week should be made by a "Game Show Host". Counselors will get appointed to announcements so they are done fun and exciting, as well as loud and clear. (auditions?)

MEAL TIMES
Theme Dinner
The lunch before the day of theme dinner the cabins will choose between 3 boxes, each one having a different meal inside. There will be a random clue as to what it is ("It has cheese in it"). The cabins will only find out what they chose when they get their meal the next night.

Lunch

Every lunch there will be Let's Make a Deal where a kid will have to bring a random item up to the front to become a contestant (i.e. red pen). They'll then get a choice of boxes. Once chosen the counselors (or other cabins) will bargain for that box with their box. Some boxes will have prizes (sweets, etc.), others will have nothing and some will have random things (like a banana).

EVENING PROGRAMS

Double Dare

"I'm going to ask you a question, and if you don't know the answer, or think the other team hasn't got a clue, you can dare them to answer it for double the dollars. But be careful, because they can always double dare you back for four times the amount, and then you'll either have to answer the question or take the physical challenge."

The host starts by asking one of the 2 teams a question. (General knowledge - can be multiple choice if need be.)

Answering the question right gives the team control of the round + points. That team now has to answer. If they don't know what the answer is or feel the other team doesn't have a clue they can DARE the other team to answer it for them. That team can answer for double points or DOUBLE DARE them back for 4x the points. Then the round starts with a physical challenge where the team with control of the round gets to choose.

Challenges:
- STUFF IT - One team member from each team is wearing overalls and 10 balloons must be stuffed into the them without popping. The team that does it the quickest wins the physical challenge gets to answer the question 1st next round.
- HUMAN WHEEL BARROW - Two kids from each team, one is the "wheel barrow" and the other the pusher, race to blow a balloon across the finish line first. The person playing the wheel barrow blows.
- BALLOON STOMP - Place a whole lot of balloons in a blocked area. Two participants from each team stomp as many as they can.
- BALLOON POP - Teams of 2 must pop as many balloons between them in 10 sec. The balloons must be placed by their tummies and they must push together to get it popped.
- COMING IN FOR A LANDING - Create box "hangers" (towers). Kids must make paper planes and write their team initials on them. They then have to fly as many paper planes as possible into the hangers in 30sec to 1min. Time can be changed.
- SPATULA TOSS - You need bread, 2 spatulas and 4 plates. Each team of 2 gets a stack of bread, a spatula and 2 plates. Team members must stand back to back. One team member stands with the stack of bread on their plate and with spatula in one hand. The other with the empty plate. The 1st team member must then flip a slice of bread with the spatula over their head to their friend who is standing back to back and they must try catch it On the plate. To make this funnier you could add peanut butter to one slice and jam to the other and try to make a "sandwich".
- HOOPSTER - Tape 2 kids' hands together (teammates). A hula hoop will be on the floor and around one kids feet - the hoop then has to go around and over both kids to the other side without using their hands.

- BOMBS AWAY - Two kids (a team) are back to back and have a basketball between them. Another ball then has to be picked up off the floor and placed on top of the basket ball without dropping it. Teams must then walk to a basket and drop the basketball (which is the bottom ball) into the basket without letting the top ball fall too.

What's in the Box?
For this evening program everything that you will use with the kids will be hidden, kids will be nominated by their cabin to come up to the front, where upon they will complete a challenge. The order in which they complete the challenge will decide the order in which they can choose a covered box. The winner getting first choice and the last person obviously getting the last box and having no choice. Inside the boxes will be Prizes, Oompa Loompas, Challenges, Fear-Factor-like-foods, etc. Once completed, repeat until everyone has had a chance to go.

Challenges can include downing a glass of water, eating competitions, endurance competitions (standing on one leg the longest, holding a stool up the longest, not blinking the longest etc.) Identifying a mystery food first (smell/taste), fastest drawing competition, etc.

Don't Forget the Lyrics Party Night
Party Night with a twist! During party night a cabin will be called up to a stage where they will
a) Name the Song
b) Name the Artist
c) Fill in the blanks that will be put up on the projector

Each a, b and c can be done all at once, then the cabin will be done, or, depending on the night , can be done at intervals.

During a Campout...
Amazing Race to the Site
Each counselor will get a set of questions and tasks that they have to complete with the kids and get photographic evidence.

Who Wants S'More?
Cabins will compete in 3 sets of challenges; the easy Biscuit Quiz, the medium Marshmallow physical challenge and the Creative Chocolate Challenge. In each challenge they will have to complete enough challenges to get enough of the food item for their cabin. There will be quiz questions, physical challenges (push-ups, running, endurance, etc.) and the creative challenge where everyone in the cabin will have to complete either Fishing, Dreamcatchers, Friendship bracelets, etc.

Game Shows (and Reality Shows that border on game shows) that can be used as inspiration for your own camp game shows include:
- Fear Factor
- American Idol
- America's Got Talent
- Minute to Win It
- Deal or No Deal
- Newlywed Game

- Jeopardy
- Double Dare
- Wheel of Fortune
- Price is Right
- Hollywood Squares
- Family Feud
- Let's Make a Deal
- Who Wants to Be a Millionaire
- Match game
- Are You Smarter Than a 5th Grader
- Name That Tune
- Survivor
- Amazing Race
- Figure It Out
- Win, Lose or Draw
- Dancing with the Stars
- Project Runway
- Shark Tank
- Treasure Hunters

It's important to get an energetic (and hopefully witty) staff person to be the game show host. Your host can make or break your game show program.

CAMP SPIRIT

One of our traditions is that we do a week long challenge for spirit. The challenge can be anything. here are some we have done:

- The group that we hear singing around camp the most
- The group picking up around camp the most
- The group that does the best camp improvement project

Or it can be a one off challenge - for example, giving them a hammer, string and a ruler and asking them to put them together and hang them off a table. We like to think of things they have to solve, because the cabins seem to love the "problem solving" more than anything else.

We'll also hide things around camp and give a clue a day for them to find the object. Sometimes it is something they already have in their group.

One time we gave them all paper and a crayon to write down all the clues. The last clue was in the crayon which told them to go to the dining hall where we had an ice cream social. (We used the "large" crayons, wrote the clue on the inside of the paper, then rolled up the paper and sealed it.)

While the challenges and hunts don't show the camper's "Spirit" like the examples I first gave, the campers really enjoy them. So now we do both. We give the campers a chance to show their camp spirit in a specific challenge like the ones above AND we have a weekly challenge or hunt that is more for fun.

The group that shows the most camp spirit by meeting the challenge best, receives a Spirit Award certificate, camp spirit pin and a camp spirit patch they can sew onto their luggage or whatever else they decide. The pins and patches were specially made for our camp.

All the other groups that meet the challenge receive the camp spirit pin as well. Sorry, there is no "Spirit Stick".

COLOR WAR

One of the biggest parts of the summer at most traditional summer camps and nearly as big of a tradition as the concept of summer camp is the color war. For several days, campers and staff members parade around camp in their team colors. Body paint, capes, mismatched socks, colored hair spray, pom-poms, and tutus are the en vogue accessories, and enthusiastic demonstrations of team pride via spirited cheers are infectious.

Although an emphasis on friendly competition geared toward giving campers an opportunity to put their camp skills to the test while exhibiting exemplary sportsmanship has prompted many camps to change the name to such things as Challenges, Tribals, College Days, and Olympics, the concept remains the same: Campers are placed onto teams and, for several days, engage in a host of activities designed to re-cap the summer—a sort of "best of" replay.

Whatever the name, the competition is often full of traditions regarded as sacred by campers and staff alike. The beginning of the games is invariably a surprise to campers and much of the staff with the reveal being is a closely guarded secret about which there is quite a bit of discussion and speculation in the days leading up to it. The breakout is unquestionably, one of the biggest events of the summer and always on everyone's list of favorite moments from the summer. Counselors are included in the action as team leaders and coaches.

The end of the competition often involves some sort of bonding activity designed to bring the teams back together as one camp family to finish out the summer because, in the end, the emphasis of a color on color contest is not whether one is on a winning team when all is said and done, but that each and every camper has had the opportunity to demonstrate what he or she has learned over the summer and, thus, gain an understanding of how each person brings something different and valuable to the camp family. Such a focus makes these types of camp activities a valuable lesson in diversity and teamwork. Everyone has a unique role on the team that directly affects the team's overall performance. For anyone—camper or staff—who has ever been a part of camps, it's the part of the summer that is undoubtedly one of the most memorable.

While the traditional Color War concept was part of a camp where the kids stayed all summer long, Color War can be adapted and played at resident camps with 1 or 2 week sessions and even day camps that are only 1 week long. You can run a Color War all in one day if you'd like, which I have seen camps do successfully. Simply create the teams earlier in the week, then on the special day start off by breaking (starting) the Color War with a bang. Give points for team and camp spirit whenever you can. Rotate the teams or age groups around to the varying competitions. In the afternoon have 1 or 2 all camp competitions. At the end of the day (or on the next day) have an awards celebration.

SummerCampPro.com

THE BEAN CUP

At our camp our best traditions seem to be a combination of good planning and happy accident. Here's an odd one, which has turned into one of our most important/fun:

We have a "Bunk Championship Trophy", which we award at the end of each week to the bunk with the most "bunk points" - which you earn all week long with good sportsmanship, camp spirit, etc. The bunk doesn't get to keep the trophy, but it's never awarded empty - there's always a special treat inside it, and the winning bunk always goes crazy cheering and posing with the trophy, and celebrates with their treat.

Well, as it happened, shortly after we started this, we had a special day, called "Bean Day" at camp - it was a little bit like Color War, but (for some inexplicable reason) we kept score with beans. So of course, all through Bean Day, everyone was completely obsessed with beans - and by the end, we all felt like we'd be happy if we never saw another bean for the rest of our lives.

So that week, when we awarded the Bunk Championship Trophy, the winning bunk got the trophy, looked inside... and found it filled with beans! They laughed, we gave them a real treat, they celebrated, and we thought that was the end of that. But for some reason, counselors and campers started calling the trophy "The Bean Cup". The name had a nice ring to it, and for the rest of the summer it stuck.

when camp ended we packed everything away for the winter. The next spring, when we were getting all the equipment ready for the upcoming camp season, we pulled out the trophy, and it brought back such great memories, that we had a little plaque made, which has been affixed to the trophy ever since. I read it during the "presentation ceremony", and all the campers always excitedly yell out the last line by heart, in the last moments before we announce the winner. The plaque says:

The All Star Israel Sports Camp Bunk Championship Trophy
"THE BEAN CUP"
Never Awarded Empty

Inevitably, at some point during the summer, the youngest campers start asking why the trophy has that name. And the counselors tell them about how, back in "the olden days" when the counselors themselves were campers, they witnessed the start of a camp tradition.

GOLDEN
With some gold spray paint you can create all sorts of trophies.

The Golden Paddle
This is awarded to the camper who wins the ping pong tournament. You can either have them take it home or you can let them hold on to it for their stay and add their name to the Golden Paddle board for that year.

Golden Dustpan
A lot of camps already do something similar to this. The Golden Dustpan is awarded daily to the cleanest cabin.

Golden Dodgeball
This is awarded to the group that wins a dodgeball tournament.

Golden Film Canister
The hardest part of this ward is finding a film canister. If you have a photography program this award would go to the best photo.

Golden Horseshoe
For those camps that have horses, the Golden Horseshoe can be given to the camper who shows the best wrangler skills, the best English rider, or the winner of a set of challenges done with a horse.

Golden Spirit Stick
The cabin that shows the most spirit, be it through cheers, song, attitude, etc. recieves this award.

Golden Pinecone
Here's a nature award that can be given for the first to complete a nature scavenger hunt, the best fairy house builder, or the winner of a nature trivia contest.

Golden Arrow
Go on a site like Etsy and buy stone carved arrowhead pendants to spray paint. Then attach them to cord for a necklace. Now you have an award for your best archers in each age group.

Golden Carabiner
Did a camper overcome their fear on the high ropes course? Who was the camper that jumped the farthest on the Pamper Pull? Who climbed the rock wall the quickest? Here's their award.

Golden GaGa Ball
Just like the Golden Dodgeball this award is given to the tournament winner(s).

If it's something the kids will take home, be sure to tell them that the object isn't really gold but that it's spray painted gold.

WHO COULD IT BE?

We put up a wanted poster on a piece of poster board. It looks like a wanted poster with a space for a picture and a reward (that changes) on the bottom.

On the first day of camp, both campers and counselors fill out a questionnaire about themselves. These questions can be easy to answer, like favorite color, name of your pet at home, etc., all the way to a little more personal, something that you learned at camp last summer, what you want to be when you grow up, etc. Then these papers are put into a big box and stored in my office. On Monday morning, I randomly pick out a paper and that is the person who is wanted for the week.

Each day there is a new clue put up about the person. The clues start out general--Monday, favorite color is purple and I am a girl, all the way to Friday which will be more specific.

Each child gets 7 guesses to use throughout the week--we keep track by the children writing their name on a piece of paper and then writing the person who they think is "Wanted".

The first person who guesses the wanted person first wins the reward of the week (a trip to Dairy Queen, free soda at lunch for the next week, extra swim time, etc.) and the reward also goes to the person who is wanted, as long as they did not tell anyone.

The next week there is a new wanted and a new reward.

STAFF SURVIVOR

This program takes place over the course of the whole summer that way ALL campers get to witness the fun and excitement. Like Survivor each week will involve reward challenges as well as elimination challenges. That's a grand total of about 18 challenges (based on a 9 week season) that you can come up with. What makes it unique at our day camp is that you have different themes each week (Canada Week, Under the Sea, Science, etc) and the challenges must correspond with those themes.

You divide your (staff) into two tribes (just for these events, the rest of the time they will be with their own individual cabin/groups). The tribe that loses each challenge will lose either a tribe member or a reward for the week. The challenges you come up with are up to you and can be individually formed for your camp. In order to separate your "tribes" you may want to have two different color staff shirts or something. I'll give you an example week from our camp.

Two Tribes: Kiwa and BGC

Reward Challenge:
Sam's Game - winning tribe receives end of week pizza party for all their kids.

Sam's game is a unique game to our camp created by our coordinator, Sam. What happens is it takes place in our gym....the counselors line up on the blue line. Whoever is leading the game calls out something in the gym...for example: "wall!". Everyone must run to a wall in the gym.... if your group is smart...they'll run to the one behind them. The last person to the wall gets eliminated (and in our version the kids all yell "Good Try").

The game continues on by calling different locations in the gym like basketball net, blue mats, black line, etc. The final challenge is often one that takes the two remaining contestants out of the gym...steps will be taken to make sure that each remaining person is from opposite tribes. Often our final challenge is to have the two people find something within the club like a certain color marker or a pillow on one of our couches.

Elimination Challenge:
Fly on the Wall
Each tribe has 10 minutes to duct tape 5 members to the wall as best as they can, the members are standing on chairs so that they don't fall. After 10 minutes we remove each chair. The team whose counselor stays up the longest win...the other team must vote out a member at lunch on Thursday...that person then goes through kids court (see below) on Friday.

The program would continue each week until the final week....On the last week you have one elimination challenge held in the middle of the week...that will narrow it down to two people. The kids at your camp will then vote on Friday for the winner. Loser gets kids court and winner gets a prize that you've put together.

This program forces your staff to work together because no one wants to lose and it also gets your kids excited because they know the competitions are fun and exciting! Work your themes into the events as well....if one of your weeks is based on Under the Sea, have the competition in the water.

Kids Court

This is the best thing that we do at camp. Every week our kids come to the coordinators and nominate staff who are breaking the rules - like swearing, running in the halls, peeing in the pool, etc....At the end of the week the kids vote on who is the worst offender and that person gets kids court. They have stuff all dumped on them like chocolate sauce, whip cream...we've honeyed and feathered staff, dressed them up like cows and made them drink milk from a bowl... what ever you can come up with. It's gross but the kids love it.

Variation:

It's never fun to be voted off of a team, even for adults. A variation of being voted off the team would be to leave it up to chance by pulling a name out of a hat or spinning a prize wheel that has all the names of the staff on that team. The name that comes up is eliminated from the team. This way there is no hard feelings among the staff. It's also easier for the kids to handle, They won't feel like their counselor is the least liked or the weakest.

Another variation from a different camp:

Each morning the staff compete in special events, then campers get to vote the staff off the island. At the end of the summer, the last staff person standing gets a $75 cash prize!

PART
7

JUST FOR STAFF

PIE MAFIA

During the course of the week staff members pay $5 to the camp director with a name of the staff individual that they want to be pied (a plate of whip cream).

Traditionally, on our last night of camp after our video highlights, the Pie Mafia completes their mission. The Pie Mafia are made up of our program staff (3 folks). Each week they make their entrance as creative as possible (driving in on a gator, dropping from the ceiling, jumping out of a trash can, etc.).

The Mission Impossible theme song is played while the Pie Mafia begin looking through the crowd for their targets, who are led up to the stage (typically 4-6 at a time) and sat in a chair.

The Pie Mafia stands behind each person and with the campers counting down, 1...2...3!, The person is pied.

The staff member who paid to get someone pied is never revealed, keeping everything anonymous, unless they choose to reveal themselves.

Money raised during the summer goes to support children in a Salvation Army orphanage in India.

*A final note. The Pie Mafia are exempt from the list as to who is being pied, that is of course until the final night of camp which we dub Pie Mafia's Revenge and three new preselected folks pie the Pie Mafia team.

STAFF "FIRST AID SUPPLIES"

In the middle of the week, the camp directors tell the new staff that they left some extra first aid supplies for them in their bedroom and ask them to put it away when they get a chance (or it's handed to them in a garbage bag and they're asked to put it away when they get a minute away from the campers).

It is SUCH a fun surprise when they go to their room or open the bag and there's cans of cold pop, chips and or chocolate bars. It's a well kept secret and once the new staff know about it, they feel like they've been let in on a super yummy secret society.

When they go back out with the campers (smiling from ear to ear) all of the returning staff are winking at them and saying "Ah, we got first aid supplies did we?"
It's really cute.

STAFF APPRECIATION

We have a weekly "contest" and reward the winner with a gift certificate for a local restaurant, coffee shop, etc.

Contests can be as easy as guessing the number of candy in a jar to a Minute to Win It game. But the favorite has been posting a picture taken at camp and having a caption contest. Some of the entries are hysterical. We then post the winning entry on a bulletin board for the entire summer.

Another staff appreciation was to do a "Secret Friend" for a week during the summer. This was like a Secret Santa, exchanging names and leaving little gifts for them throughout the week. We had a limit of $5.00 but many gifts were made or found and didn't cost anything.

Staff Praise Walls are also great to do. After a week of camp, ask parents to email you with any prise for their child's counselor, or other staff, that can be posted on the Praise Wall. You'll be surprised at the wonderful things parents will have to say and how great they think the idea of a Praise Wall is. The staff love to see their name mentioned on there.

THE STAFF ENCOURAGEMENT GNOME

Near the end of the summer we took a gnome (a little one found at Wal-Mart) and duct taped a slot/envelope at the bottom of it. The goal was to pass the gnome around to all of the camp staff in a unique and creative way, with an encouraging note stuck in the little slot. Every staffer could only get it once, and they had to pass it on quickly and creatively.

We had staff put them in odd places for the other to find. One person attached the gnome to the archery target for the archery instructor. One floated the gnome on a raft in the pool. Another gave it to campers to give. There were many other ways as well. This provided encouragement, creativity and just added something different to the end of the summer.

In order to keep track of who already got it and who hasn't, have the program director keep a list. When a staffer gets the gnome they must let the program director know so he/she can cross off their name.

The encouraging notes should be personal, not generic like, "You're doing a fine job this week."

Want to get the campers involved? Give each group their own gnome. Write the group's counselor's name on it so you know which group it belongs to. Any camper from the group can write a note for a counselor and give it to them in a fun way. The counselor of the group must approve the note before it goes out. You don't want some prankster to write something rude or hurtful. After the staffer finds the gnome and reads the note they return it to that group, hopefully with a smile on their face.

STAFF BOOSTERS

Summer Camp should definitely have a sense of adventure and anticipation about what's coming up next. Staff are essential in helping to keep the fun-ergy (Yep...that's a word) sustained all summer long.

One way we can help to keep the staff motivation is to do energy boosters throughout the summer. Our staff take breaks in the staff lounge, so each week the management team is taking turns to decorate the lounge with different themes and leave treats. That sounds simple (and it is) but the staff also need to have a sense of novelty and wonder. Anticipating what treasures await them in the staff lounge week to week is a great way to lift spirits and say thanks for a job well done.

We also leave care packages on each camp counselors door step (or mail them) before camp begins with a prop for each weeks theme. For instance, if we are hosting a Glow in the Dark Party they will get Glow In the Dark Sticks. If we are also hosting a Twisted Fairy Tales week each counselor will get a crown, wand or cape in their care package. It's a box full of fun so that the counselors have what they need to help Jazz it up!

POCKET PATCH

At the camp where I work, we have a special room in our main lodge just for our counselors.

On the wall in that room is what we call a 'Pocket Patch'. It's basically a large piece of fabric with pockets sewn onto it. Each staff member and volunteer is assigned a pocket each week (we use paper clips to pin name tags onto the pockets).

The Pocket Patch is a mail system for everyone to write letters of encouragement or to give small gifts to each other. It's wonderful to find something in your pocket when you are having a particularly hard day!

CAMP NAMES and CEREMONY

Does your staff use camp names? If not, they should. Camp names are fun for the staff, the campers and even the parents. I would always introduce myself to parents with my real name as well as my camp name. About 90% of them would use my camp name when speaking with me.

If you're worried that it may seem disingenuous or deceitful to use a "fake" name, then have your staff introduce themselves to their campers with their real names and then their camp names. Let the campers decide which name they want to use. I guarantee you that the campers will almost always prefer to use their counselor's camp name instead of their real name.

So, how does a person get a camp name? Are they given one by other staff or do they choose their own? I feel that most nicknames that are given to us when we were kids stem from something embarrassing we did or an attribute that we don't necessarily care for about ourselves. We didn't get to choose our real names. We didn't get to choose our childhood nicknames. So, I figure we should be able to choose our camp names.

Of course, I tell my staff that their name must have some meaning for them. Just because they like apples they shouldn't choose Apple as their camp name. On the other hand, if they are from The Big Apple, New York, then the name "Apple" seems appropriate.

THE CEREMONY

Since my staff get to choose their own camp name, and I wanted the whole idea of using camp names to be special, I decided to create a "Camp Name" Ceremony.

The ceremony takes place in a separate room on the last day of our staff training week. Any return staff who already have their camp names start off in the ceremonial room.

The room is dark with candles all around. Each person is given a percussion instrument like a drum, cabasa, claves, cow bell, rainstick, rattle, tambourine or wood block. Each new staff member is brought into the room blindfolded one at a time. The others wait in another room where they cannot hear what is going on.

When the new staff person is guided into the ceremonial room the return staff quietly start a rhythm with their instruments and sing the fish tank chant on Mount Wannahockaloogie from the movie Finding Nemo. "Hoo-Ha-Ha-Ha-Hoo-Ha-Ha-Ha!" As the new person is walked up to the front of the room the chant gets louder and louder. Once the person has reached the front, the director makes a hand motion and everyone stops chanting and drumming at once. If timed correctly, and everyone is paying attention, the immediate stop of chanting and drumming is very cool.

The new staff member is asked to take a knee or kneel. Then they are asked to reveal their camp name. Once they do everyone in the room silently gives a thumbs up or thumbs down. It is the director who gets the final say, however. If the director does not accept the name they must give an alternate. Another vote is taken. If the alternate is not accepted they are ushered out and must come up with a third choice with the help of a return staff member.

However, if the name IS accepted, the director uses a fake sword (we use a boffer) and "knights" the person, then says, "Rise, (their camp name)."

Before they take off their blindfold a veteran staff person uses face paint to make one line on their cheek which represents their first year. All return staff have multiple lines on their cheeks as well, representing how many years (or summers) they have worked at camp.

Once they take off their blindfold they are given their t-shirts and a welcome bag. Then they find a seat and participate in the rest of the ceremony. The next person is now guided into the room and the chanting begins again.

There is also a person in the corner of the room that is recording everyones camp names. We use this list to make new name tags for the staff and for the daily camp schedule. They get their new name tags on the first day of camp.

At some point we would like to get a bunch of cloaks for all the return staff to wear. Currently we only have 5, but we use them all. It really adds to the effect. Staff never forget this ceremony. Each year we add something new like another robe/cloak, a cool lighting effect, a new drum, etc.

We have also been thinking about adding Venetian style masks. Return staff can get their own unique masks before coming to camp and new staff will be given generic black ones.

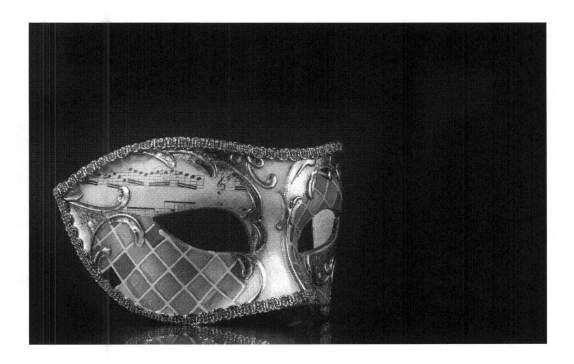

PART
8

OTHER

POLAR BEAR SWIM

One of the highlights of summer camp at Drift Creek is the daily Polar Bear Swim! We are an overnight, week-long camp in the Siuslaw National Forest of Oregon. A pristine, but frigidly cold, mountain stream surrounds our grounds. Each morning, eager swimmers arise early to gather at the creekside. We have a competition, and cabins that have the highest percentage of polar bear swim participants receive the privilege of hosting "Boris" for the day. Boris is now a 21-year old, very well worn, bandaged eye stuffed polar bear!

The polar bear swimmers stand by the creekside and jump in one cabin at a time. Some campers jump in just long enough to get wet while others swim to the other side in order to climb up on a rock and then jump back in. But before jumping in they collectively sing:

It's summer time at Drift Creek
And it's 40 degrees below
The polar bears are swimming
Because they love it so

So early in the morning
They break through the ice and snow
It's summer time at Drift Creek
AND IT'S 40 DEGREES BELOW!!! BRRRRR! (and then they all jump into the water!)

Then at the end of the week, every camper who goes polar bearing EVERY morning receives a certificate and a pack of wintermint gum or peppermint patties (some kind of candy associated with coolness.....) They also take a group picture with Boris on the last day of camp so there is a lot of hype around it. We have one person on staff who has not missed a single morning of polar bearing in 10 years of camping!!!

TELL ME ABOUT YOU

Our biggest hit this summer was around the campfire. Our camp is for 5th-8th graders only (The Middle School Age). As you know this group can be tough to keep focused, but loves to share ideas and thoughts about themselves. So here's our outstanding moment this summer....

It was just getting dark and our campfire gathering was starting. The kids were very much into cooking s'mores (who isn't) and I felt it was time to start the story telling. As expected, getting the kids attention was difficult so I was so surprised when I started the theme for the night and got immediate response.... Tonight's Theme is "Tell me a story about yourself..."

We started the night with, "Tell me a story where you were really scared, not mostly scared or sort of scared but really scared. It has to be true and the crowd will vote if it was Hot or Not at the end."

From scary we went to "Favorite Funny Moments about your counselor....." As you can imagine the kids loved to spill the beans on silly, smelly, clumsy moments with the big kid in charge.

From there we moved onto letting the kids pick the next topic. Before I knew it, over an hour flew by and there was no letting up in the fun.

And that's when we brought in the Neon Rain (break a 100 or 200 glow sticks and have a group hiding in the shadows. As you begin telling a story about one dark and scary night, when all of a sudden you saw a flash (in comes 1 glow stick). Continue to spin the yarn, making it personal to the camp/campers or your home town/school. One flash leads to another and as you build the story in excitement and anticipation, lead up to the climax with the remaining 150 or so glow sticks thrown in the air to make neon rain.

Some story themes that have worked for me in the past: A science teacher (use someone's real name) who had an experiment go out of control; A walk in the woods when you came across small creatures (dare I say aliens) fighting with light sabers. Or, the time you tripped upon a magician training fire flies to perform....

Needless to say, this night will remain with me from the many (over 20 years) of Summer Time Story Telling around a Fire.

THEMED TRAILS

I have been experimenting with themed trails at camp. I find that many of our younger campers do not enjoy hiking because they dislike the mosquitoes and deer flies, or their parents have them terrified about getting Lyme disease from ticks. I decided that it was time to create a distraction.

"ANIMAL TRACKER" TRAIL

We attached animal track rubbing plates (from Nature Watch), a laminated picture, and a few facts on each animal to wooden signs. I then screwed the signs to metal fence posts, which were spaced along the trail. Then, using animal track resins purchased from Nature Watch, I made tracks in cement, painted them brown, and hid them along the path.

The campers are given booklets and a crayon for taking rubbings of the tracks, and then they have to find the footprints for that animal. The campers walk eagerly to find the next post. Yet once they are there, they have to slow down to take turns for the rubbing and for finding the animals prints. This forces them to stop and take a look around them, often making other discoveries.

At the end of the season, the signs and footprints are collected and stored. This idea works great for our regular campers and for our nature education program with visiting elementary schools.

TREE IDENTIFICATION

Find a trail that has the most variety of trees along it. Place signs near the tree that needs to be identified. See if they can find the trees' seeds underneath the canopy. Campers can take leaf and bark rubbings.

One year I had my campers, take bark rubbings in a patchwork pattern on a large sheet of paper. In the center of the paper, they wrote diamante poems about trees, and then they framed them with bark of trees we had already cut down. They had something really special to take home.

STORY TRAIL

Cut apart and laminate a book to make a story trail. They read the next page as they find it. My favorite book for young campers is *Dirt Boy* by Erik Jon Slangerup. It is about a little boy who is tired of being clean, runs off into the woods, and finds a giant. The book could change every week.

FAIRY TRAIL

Pick out a trail that has fascinating stumps, unusual tree trunks and moss for the fairy trail. Have campers construct homes, dishes, furniture, and paths for fairies out of natural materials they find on the forest floor. Campers will have fun walking along the trail to see what other campers have done. Hang tinkling wind chimes out of sight. There are some really neat fairy rubbing plates as well for them to collect.

AMPHIBIAN AND REPTILE TRAIL

We have some wetlands and two vernal pools on our property where campers love to catch frogs. This trail leads to this area, and they can learn about the creatures they will find along the way.

FOLKLORE TRAIL
Our campers have been making loads of forts in the woods. Sometimes, it is mysterious to walk by these groupings of abandoned shelters. We build on to local tales and make up a few of our own.

There is a tree where we hang percussion and chime type instruments for them to play as background effects for some of the storytelling. I may use geocaches to hide the folklore tales for this trail.

MAKE UP YOUR OWN (MUYO)

At our camp we have a program called Make Up Your Own (MUYO). When the campers come to this area, they are provided with a variety of materials - such as boxes, milk crates, and balls.

They then must come up with a game or activity as a group that uses the supplies provided. This new activity works relatively well. The main factor on whether it succeeds or not is the staff's participation. If they are excited and into it, the campers love it, but if they are unenthusiastic, the campers do not buy into the concept.

The days that campers enjoy MUYO the most are on the very hot days. We provide them with a hose, buckets, sponges, and tubes. Some groups design mini water parks, others design dunk tanks, and many have sponge water fights.

This program needs some forethought to run smoothly. The equipment that will be used each day needs to be planed for ahead of time. On the days when we do not have time to plan out the equipment, the campers are not as engaged or enthused. If you have time to plan and gather the materials needed and have good staff buy in, the campers will really enjoy this unusual camp activity.

Steps:
1. During staff training introduce MUYO. We have the staff participate in the area which help them buy into it.
2. Plan out the different materials you would like to use for the program. Ensure that there is a variety and that new things are added or provided when the campers have MUYO subsequent times.
3. Explain to the campers when they come to the area, or have their counselor explain, the different materials provided and that they must as a group come up with a game, build something, or do some activity with what is provided.
4. Let the campers have free reign over their creation and watch them have fun. You should participate in the activities but don't direct or suggest components unless safety is a concern. The point of this is for them to have a time of free play and stimulate their creativity.
5. At the end of the time period, have the campers put all the supplies back to where they belong.

When we ran MUYO, each group had approximately an hour to create, play and clean up.

If the campers come up with a great game consider adding it to your games program for all campers. Another thing you can do is ask the MUYO groups to use the materials and come up with a challenge that will be used in the Camp Olympics at the end of the week. This gives the activity a purpose and the campers will be inspired to create an awesome challenge since they know that other campers will be playing it. Let them know that the best ones will be used in future Camp Olympics.

MILESTONE AWARDS AT CAMP

Many camps celebrate the number of years a camp or staff person have been coming to camp. Here are the ways four different camps handle this.

YEAR PINS

We have pins for campers or staff who have been coming to camp for either 5,10,15,20 years. This is presented at the final campfire for the week in front of the whole camp. Then the camper/ staff member is to share a memory from their days at camp.

5 YEAR BREAKFAST

One of our most popular traditions is our "5 year breakfast." We are a day camp, and the 6th week of the summer, we invite all campers and staff who are in at least their 5th year at camp to join us for breakfast during the first period of the day.

As a day camp, this is the only time we serve breakfast during the summer. At breakfast, we give a special sweatshirt to everyone in their 5th summer and a blanket to everyone in their 10th. It never ceases to amaze me how many parents tell me that their campers have to return for their 5th year so that they can attend the breakfast.

10 YEAR DINNER

We have a celebration for our 4 year campers, and recognize 6 years and 8 years with gifts. We also have a really special 10-year dinner for everyone who has been at camp 10 years or more. Additionally, we give out a felt star patch every summer for them to put on their patch pillow, so they can count their number of summers by the number of stars on their pillow.

PADDLES

We do 10 year paddles for anyone (camper, staff, volunteer) who has given 10 years to our camps. They are wooden paddle cut-outs (about 2.5 feet long) and we router and then burn each person's name (and, if applicable, camp name) into their own paddle and then hang it in the rafters of the main lodge. We have been doing this tradition for 12 or 13 years now and have about 200 paddles up (I believe we got the idea from Camp Winona in Bracebridge, ON). Helps with long-term retention (kids and staff want to keep coming back so they can get that paddle up there!), as well as recognizing those who have given a lot of time, leadership and service to our camps. It's also inexpensive (we pay for the wood, a volunteer cuts them out and my co-director routers and burns the names in them) and an incredible, permanent, way to share in people's camp legacy.

Here is a picture of those receiving their 5 year blankets at Gold Arrow Camp and a picture of the coin given after 10 years to ESF Summer Camps campers.

ACKNOWLEDGMENTS

At afternoon line-up we do something called "Acknowledgments". Campers are given a few minutes to acknowledge one another for doing something above and beyond, reaching a goal or being helpful. For example, "I want to acknowledge John. It took him three tries and he did not get discouraged. Today he made it up to the top of the climbing wall" and "I want to acknowledge Mary. She knew I was upset when I didn't get the lead in the camp play. She found me after I walked out of the theater and helped calm me down and put a smile on my face".

The person making the acknowledgment and the person being acknowledged both stand.

It may take a few days for campers to understand what is appropriate to say, but it is pretty powerful when it takes off.

CAMPER RECOGNITION

Below is how two different camps do camper recognition.

We do as many things as possible to recognize campers (and staff) for achievements, participation, etc. One of our methods is a bead program.

BEADS

Everyone makes a leather name tag their first day on camp and we begin giving out beads as soon as possible. We use pony beads of all sorts. We have several beads that a camper can get just for "showing up" -- such as one for attending camp, one for spending one night at camp ("old timer"), and different team beads for special events. Other beads are given for improved behavior, cooperation with staff, friendship, sportsmanship, specific achievements in skill areas (boating, swimming, crafts, athletics, etc.). Our campers bring their name tags and beads back year after year, and add to them each year.

COMPASS AWARDS

Several years ago we found Compass Awards (www.compassawards.com). Return-  ing campers who are at least 9 years old are given the opportunity to work toward earning a patch (we use the canoe version) and the smaller award patches to go on it. There are written standards for what has to be accomplished in order to qualify for each one. Areas where award patches can be won include: drama, archery, crafts, canoeing, swimming, honor camper, teamwork, nature, service, athletics, OLS, etc.

BEAD PROGRAM - BEADS FROM FITNESS FINDERS

A motivator we have found to be successful is a Bead Program; I actually found this idea on your website. We have modified it to meet our program needs: we will provide beads for making positive behavioral choices. For example when a child goes out of the way to help another or picks up a random piece of garbage they might get recognized for it. We do pony beads for Behavior and different colors represent different behaviors. We also have "Theme Weeks" through out the summer and each week has its own bead which the children all look forward to earning.

We started this program 2 summers ago and actually have children that still have the beads. I order the themed beads from FitnessFinders.net. Some examples we have used is during Science Week we do a "Brain Bead", Time Travelers week we use a "World Bead" and for Game Show week we used a "Ribbon Bead".

TRADING POST COINS

Our day camp serves children ages 5-12. We like to reward campers and staff for a job well done. Custom "happy camper" stickers are presented at morning assembly every day to those campers nominated by their staff for being kind, picking up trash, showing great team spirit, etc. Children save them like treasure. This past year we had coins minted to help us in this area. The coins cost $.25 per piece. This is how we use the coins to enhance the camp experience.

Staff rewards:
Every day, the staff are rewarded with a $1 Trading Post coin for arriving to work on time. The coins are passed out in the morning staff meeting as they come in the door.

Trading Post Novelty:
The coins are sold in the Trading Post. Some children buy them for souvenirs, and others exchange their money for coins just to spend later.

Marketing:
We also pass out the coins to the children who come for the day with their school on a field trip. If they sign up to come to camp, they get to spend it. Regardless, it gives them something solid to bring home to mom and dad. Paper is so easily discarded, but kids love the coins.

Birthday gifts:
Our next plan is to send out birthday cards with a coin inside. They can keep it for a memento or spend it next year. Our cost ranges from $.25 to $.60 depending on whether they keep it or redeem it.

It is amazing how such a small thing can create such excitement!

The vendor for the coins is American Changer in Ft. Lauderdale, FL.

SHARING STORIES OF THE IMPACT OF CAMP

Last year we began to focus more on the meaning of and tradition of CAMP. During our staff orientation we began to focus on this by sharing our camp stories (the YMCA has a new initiative about sharing your impact stories, so we applied it to camp).

The directors and leadership team began orientation with their Y stories-when they became involved with the camp, how long they have been there and in what capacities, and how their time at the camp had impacted their lives.

Next the leadership team shared impact stories about the children and families we serve. Many new staff were amazed to hear such thoughtful, emotional stories about what they had originally thought of as "just a camp job!"

When it was time for the rest of the staff to share their personal impact stories and or stories about children and families they had impacted with camp there were tears everywhere! Many of us were amazed to learn how long some of the staff had been there!

One staff member had started as a preschool camper! Another staff member shared that she was currently in foster care and just from the camp orientation she already felt like she had a place to belong and that people around her cared about her! And she was not the only staff member in foster care!

We were amazed at how much our staff shared with each other - some of whom knew no one else there at the start of training.

I think these reflection exercises really helped bring the staff together. We formed a solid support group for each other during orientation. This coming summer we will build on the success of this program and include the campers in a weekly reflection at our final closing program each week. Focusing on how camp made you feel will help the campers keep those great memories with them!

GO GET THE SHERIFF

The following ideas are based how well your local law enforcement agencies will work with you. The San Bernardino County Sheriff's Dept. has been invaluable and creative.

We did a spy camp 3 years ago and called in help from our county Sheriff's department. There was a fake crime scene, a body line taped off on the floor an various elements to help the kids figure out what happened. The CSI team came in and taught the kids different ways to collect and analyze evidence. They let them lift fingerprint from ceramic tiles. Then they took them to the crime scene, collected evidence and tried to solve the crime.

Two years ago, we had a near tragedy in our community lake and a boy almost drowned. Our theme for camp that year was Castaway Island, so again with the help of our Sheriff's dept.(have you noticed that they are really nice) the search and rescue team simulated a drowning rescue. They flew a helicopter in over the lake and dropped divers. The local fire dept. rolled in and it was really neat for the kids to see how a rescue would happen. Especially since the child who nearly drowned was accidentally found on the bottom of the lake when someone stepped on him. Of course, the kids then got to have their picture taken in the helicopter and they had tons of questions.

Our San Bernardino County Sheriff's Dept. is wonderful, I hope that everyone has a department that will work with them. It is a great resource for us when our theme can incorporate them and they love to help us be creative.

I am considering a western camp this year, if I do that, I will be calling the Applevalley Sheriff's Posse. They are a volunteer horseback division of the search and rescue team.

COMMUNITY HELP

We make our camp special and magical by inviting in the community to be part of our camp themes. This would include inviting the police and fire departments to celebrate hero week, having local mascot characters come for monster week, and inviting parents with special talents to come in and share (guitar, singing, magic etc.). Utilizing all these free opportunities already available and tying them into the weekly theme helps to create a fun, community minded experience.

Each community has their own pool to draw from, and we have found that most businesses and community members jump at the chance to share in the camp day and be part of our themes. It does take a community to raise a child.

Here are some additional ideas for using your community to help create a memorable experience at camp...

- If there is a military base close by ask them to come for a visit. They may be willing to bring in special vehicles, give an outdoor survival workshop, or lead a morning run.
- Do you have space to land a helicopter? Hospitals, local news stations, corporations, police departments, military and helicopter tour companies are all places you can check out to make this happen.
- Bring in big and/or cool vehicles for the campers to check out. Contact construction companies, fire departments, hot rod clubs, motorcycle clubs, public works, the National Guard, etc. to see if they would be willing to come by.
- Contact a local radio station to come in with their event van and play some music.
- Find out if a local theater group would be willing to come in and do a quick play, speak with the campers about acting and maybe do some stage combat. If you have a theme for the week they might be willing to dress for it.
- Is there a local band that would come in and do a free show?

KITCHEN RAIDS

Raccoons aren't the only ones that can raid a kitchen. At our camp the older campers have the option to participate in their own kitchen raid. This is when, at night, after the they are suppose to be settling down into bed, campers leave their cabin with their leaders and "sneak" into the kitchen, where preplanned (by their leaders) snacks are left out for them to take! This is a favorite of mine as they can be done in so many ways.

Some cabins like to be "caught" or scared by other camp staff, others preferred not to be or it to be lighter outside, etc. The best part is planning this as a cabin! It really gets all of the campers involved by choosing the path they are taking to the kitchen, who is doing what, or a special camp staff member who will join them. It is so exciting for them and a highlight of the week!

It's important that the campers understand that they are not breaking the rules, that this is a privilege for them and it has been authorized. That's not to say that you can't weave a story of how the director's wife doesn't agree with campers being out of bed so late, that if she catches you there will be some scolding. In order to avoid that the group must be careful not to get caught outside. Once they are in the dining hall they will be safe.

One of the things that is fun to do as well is leave a card or note for the cooks thanking them for leaving food out for their raid and for doing such a great job with the camp food. Kitchen staff love to be recognized. The more thanks they get the more they are willing to do special things for the campers and staff.

FAIRY TALE NIGHT

We did something called fairy tale night where we dressed the staff of our youngest campers up and spread them out throughout our site. We woke our youngest campers up around 11:00pm and created a story featuring Humpty Dumpty who led them around camp to meet some of his fairy tale friends.

At every station our fairy tale characters came to life and explained why they were at camp that night (to help Humpty Dumpty).

At the end of the tour we give every camper a piece of candy as a token of the fairy tale characters appreciation.

The key to the program is making sure to completely deny it the following day and clean the area thoroughly so there is no sign of what happened the previous night once the campers wake up the following morning.

TIME CAPSULE

Every couple of years, we have our Leadership Challenge program (freshmen and sophomores in high school) put together a time capsule and bury it on property.

They put items that they made or found at camp and decorate the container. They decide where to bury it and we make a map showing where it will be and keep that in the office.

On the 10 anniversary of each time capsule we attempt to contact the campers that were a part of that time capsule and invite them back to dig it up. It's always fun to watch them open the capsule and go through it's contents.

Afterwards, we have a special "welcome back" luncheon for them. This happens right after the summer season end so that we still have staff available to cook and to run activities if the group wants to participate in any of them.

Here is a list of items that can be placed in the time capsule...
- Letters to yourself or a fellow camper
- Camp T-Shirt with everyone's signatures
- Camp buttons and lanyard
- Photos of the group
- A recording of the group with a message for their future selves
- A notebook of funny things that happened during camp
- Camp brochure

There are certain materials that you should not place in your capsule since they break down over time and the gases could ruin your items. Those items are anything rubber and perishable and edible items. Also, make sure your store your photos correctly.

WWII Time Capsule

MAIL NINJAS

Mail is delivered once a day at lunch time. Mail call can sometimes be disappointing for those kids who never get any mail. Enter the Mail Ninjas! If you aren't going to get a letter, at least you'll be entertained.

As soon as their theme song comes on (Inner Ninja by Classified), the Mail Ninjas start to pop up in windows around the building. They enter the Dining Hall giving high fives and doing ninja moves.

As names are called, the Mail Ninjas deliver to that camper while doing somersaults and other ninja moves.

On the last day, the Mail Ninjas hide in the Dining Hall during lunch and bust out of their hiding spot, surprising the kids and delivering the mail.

Everyone loves the Mail Ninjas! They start to sing along to the song, singing "...the Mail Ninjas!" They dance their best Ninja moves while the song plays and the mail is delivered!

CAMP BUDDIES

I went to a YWCA camp more than 40 years ago..... my mother even attended the same camp before me! Most kids attended by-the-week, but some families were able to send their girls for 2 or more sessions. Even though that camp no longer exists, I have unbelievable memories from my summer days there in southern Ohio; which encouraged my love of teaching, camp counseling, and now directing summer day camps for both boys and girls. When it comes to camp, I am still a (big) kid!

I recall an evening activity, which was held early in the week - Monday or Tuesday night probably. We had "upper camp" (the older kids) and "lower camp" (the younger ones).

After dinner, pulled from a hat; names were announced (one girl from upper camp was paired up with one girl from lower camp). This appeared to be random, but I suppose it could be pre-arranged by the camp staff . The "camp buddies" spent that evening activity time together, and could take part in a number of different camp games, arts and crafts, land sports, archery, tennis, etc. (The counselors were each "manning" a learning or play station, and the kids were able to cruise around on their own with their new buddy.) This activity provided opportunity for two strangers to get acquainted with each other, and encouraged week-long communication by way of notes, candy from the camp store, sitting together at announcements or activities, etc.

I remember my very first summer, I was maybe 8 years old, and that "Sarah" was my assigned camp buddy. I still remember that she had 7 brothers! She was older and wiser than me; and had been coming to the camp for a few years. Sarah was a seasoned camper, and told me about some of the fun memories she had, and was able to educate me about some of the camp fun to come. I remember looking up to her and thinking she was so cool!

At lunch one day, we got to sit with our camp buddies! We normally sat with our own cabin groups. I remember that during rest period, we could draw pictures or write notes to our buddies, and I guess they were delivered after the evening meal when mail was distributed. We were able to purchase novelties from a camp store, and we could buy little trinkets for our buddies.

At the end of the week, campers could 'introduce' and share stories or funny things that happened during the week with their buddy. We even made wood picture frames which we wood burned "Best Buddies" or something like that. Each camper received a black and white Polaroid picture of them self with their buddy! I think too, that we were encouraged to be pen pals, because I kept in touch with Sarah for a time after that.

A few years later, when the tables were turned and I was in upper camp with a younger buddy; I remember the feeling of pride and experience when getting to know a younger camper. Returning campers always looked forward to getting a camp buddy, and the newbies connected with somebody that perhaps they might never have gotten the chance to know.

BUTTON TRADING

This is a mash-up of how two camps do a button trading program.

Button trading might not be for everyone, but this summer it's for you! If you get into this, the kids will too! Its a great conversation starter and a way to get some of the less athletic kids excited too.

We have buttons (size 1.25) for EVERYTHING. Staff, buildings, activities, favorite camp foods, inside camp jokes…literally everything and more.

It has been a HUGE addition to our camp culture and is actually a pretty decent moneymaker as well in our camp store. We sell the buttons for $1. We have a Monday Starter Pack Special where they get 5 buttons, a lanyard and instructions on how the program works for $5. Then after that, every button is $1. The buttons are made for pennies once you have the button maker and begin to buy/sell buttons.

Staff will receive a lanyard too (with a name tag), with 10 buttons (that belong to camp). The buttons on their lanyard do not belong to them, but they can purchase their own buttons at a discount. If a camper wants to trade with a staffer, the staffer MUST trade with them the one that the camper wants (similar to how Disney does with their trading pins). If it's on their staff lanyard it is free game for trading. Campers, however, are not required to trade if they don't want to.

Staff Rules
- Staff Must wear their lanyard/nametag on opening and closing days
- Staff Must wear or have their lanyard on their backpack all other days
- Staff Must have 10 buttons on their lanyard at all times (lost buttons can be replaced)
- Staff can switch buttons off their lanyard as they please for their own collection as long as they keep 10 on the lanyard
- Staff may not give free buttons away without permission from the Summer Camp Director

Camper Rules
- Campers may not trade "Non-Camp " buttons with staff members
- Campers may only trade during appropriate times (not in the middle of an A/O game, while someone is lifeguarding, in the bathroom, when you are running late)
- Campers may not do "temporary" trades
- Campers may trade each other any combination of trades up to a 3 for 1 trade, etc.

FYI - We put our website tiny on the edge to mark them as ours. While we made buttons for all the activities, logos, events and games, using a lot of clip art, in the end the hot sellers were weird ones like camp dogs, things that didn't make sense like "glow stick cheeseburger" or inside jokes. The more types you make the better.

They cost about $.10 to make, so while we sell them for $1 each some camps may want to sell them for $.50 each.

We purchased our machine from American Button Machines. I wondered how it would carry over for the 2nd year, but it was great because all of the sudden we had "vintage" buttons that were no longer being made that campers brought back. We even had "immunity buttons."

Buttons from Hidden Valley Camp

Found on Etsy

Busy Beaver Button Company

MAGICAL MOMENTS

One of the biggest changes that we made was adding the "creating magical experiences" to our mission statement for camp. Placing these three words in such a prominent place allowed us to focus on being very intentional about it.

The challenge that we gave each and every counselor, and what we held them to by the way, was to each week have that "one" moment that they did something for their campers that was outside of the "norm." It couldn't be an activity that we already offer at camp. It had to be special, creative, and have a surprise element to it.

Each staff meeting we'd ask our counselors to report on if they had completed their "magical moment" yet. To this day, I still hear from parents, not about zip line or swimming, or the great evening programs, but about that thing the counselor did with their cabin.

Here are a few magical moments that I saw our counselors create for their campers:
- Late night camp kitchen raids
- Bringing all of their sleeping bags and pillows to the flagpole before any arrived and giving their appearance that they slept there all night
- Placing a huge blanket over their dining hall table and eating under the table as if they were in a cave
- Nighttime camp store raid
- Organizing every cabin to surround the director's house at 5 a.m. and sing a song
- Driving to Dairy Queen on their time off to buy ice cream for their cabin

What are some of the ways your camp could do very little things that make a lasting impression?

CAMPER ROUNDTABLE

At our camp the campers have a voice. At the beginning of the session one camper is chosen as a representative for the cabin group. At a specific time all representatives gather together with the leadership staff to discuss camp.

At the first meeting everyone introduces themselves and the staff person leading the meeting explains the responsibility each camper has. He or she tells them that they are to go back to their group and ask them what they like about camp and what they would like improved on or changed. The representatives are to come back the following day at the same time to give everyone a report.

On day 2 there are discussions about what campers like about camp and what they would like changed. The campers feel they have a real voice in what happens at camp. It also gives us feedback about what we are doing right and where we might need to improve. Later in the week the leadership staff put certain ideas and plans, based on what the representatives have reported, to a vote. Each representative gets an anonymous vote. The staff do not as they chose what to vote on. If a project or event is voted in then it starts immediately. If an activity or something is voted out then it stops immediately.

As you might expect, the older campers are the most vocal. We get a real feel for who the movers and shakers are and who might make great future staff.

The whole program gives the campers a sense of ownership and many of our improvements at camp have come from our roundtables.

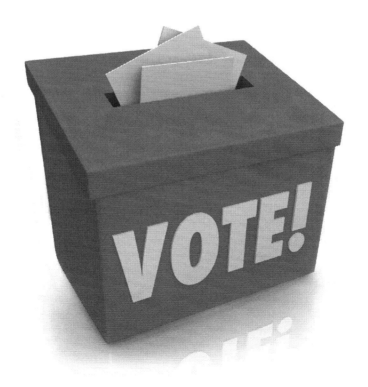

ULTIMATES

We have Ultimates- which are choice activity periods for our campers. They have 2 in the morning and 2 in the afternoon, so they choose 4 for the week that they want to do.

The offerings are a diversity of programs from sports, arts, nature, drama, specially themed activities, etc. The choices come from the counselors. They get to choose what they want to offer. We have a list or they can propose a new activity. They do three or four different offerings each week. We make sure we have a few of each type in each period, so it is not heavy on one or more type of activity.

The activities are progressive throughout the week- Example; Basketball- would start off with easy drills and skills and work throughout the week to end with a mini tournament. Mask Making- would start with drawings and finish with a mask to take home. The mask is not done in the first class. Some other offerings like Ball Mania- have a different ball game that is played each day they meet. No two Ultimates are alike.

How we manage the choices...
The counselors put in their request for what they would like to teach each Wednesday, and our Program Coordinator goes through the offerings and comes up with a schedule to balance the different types for the following week. Counselors have to submit a description and the progression of activities for any new offerings not on the list.

How we manage the sign-ups for campers:
On Mondays, the first day of camp each week, in the morning we hold an Ultimate Show- like a fashion show of the offerings. Each counselor gets up and displays and gives a quick description of their Ultimate and what they will be doing. Counselors will use props, or do short skits to show off their Ultimates. After each counselor is done they go to a predetermined spot in the room or in another room, like a gymnasium.

After the show, each camper has an index card with their name on it and four spots to fill in- Period 1, 2, 3 & 4. They go around the room and look for the Ultimate and counselor they want to sign up with. They get in line, when they reach the front of the line they have their card filled out with the name of the Ultimate on the period that it is being offered, the counselor then writes the child's name on the roster for that Ultimate, which can have a maximum number to it, so when the counselor fills up their roster for an Ultimate it is full and no one else can sign up.

After the camper has filled their card with their 4 choices, they hand it in and head off to a game being offered that we can add and grow with more children arriving- sharks & minnows. for instance.

We found if campers don't get the Ultimate they wanted, because it is full, they move on to another line to sign up. It is a whole different mentality then not getting your 1st or second choice when you fill out a card and hand it in and the next day you find out what you received. They are empowered to make their choices and get the card filled up. They know what they are going to get as it is happening and when they are done they know and are happy with it. Our Jr. counselors and CIT's help the campers with choices and finding what they want.

Next...
You will have index cards with campers names on them and which activity they are in each period, so alphabetize these and place them on a ring and if you need to find a camper during the day, go to the cards, look up the camper and the period you are in and that is where the child is- no retyping or making up a list.

You will also have a roster of who is in each activity, from the names that the counselors were writing down. Make copies of these for your records and give one to the counselor for them to take attendance with. We have snack between each of our Ultimate periods, so campers can get with their new counselor to go off to their new Ultimate. Our snack time is around our flag pole or inside in inclement weather. Good time for all camp announcements and such.

What are the benefits:
- Counselors get to choose what they would like to teach- Happy Counselors
- Campers get to choose what they want to take- Happy Campers
- Admin Staff doesn't have to assign campers, make lists, or do any paperwork- Happy Admins
- Happy Staff, Happy Counselors, Happy Campers = Happy and Fun Camp!

MAJORS and MINORS

Scheduling: We have a system of Majors/Minors. The kids are allowed to choose up to 4 majors and 8 minors. It is easiest if they fill out all 8 minors to fill their schedules. They send these into us before camp along with their other paperwork.

Majors are programs they do every day. Minors are every other day. We take all the forms and plug them into excel and begin scheduling. Usually when the schedules are finished I end up with a couple that would be missing an activity to fill a period or two.

The kids come on Sunday evening so that allows me to meet with the ones that I am missing activities from and fill in the gaps before the schedules are printed and handed out Monday morning. We then have one change night on Tuesday night (at this point they have already gone through one Monday schedule and Tuesday schedule) for them to change any periods they did not like. On this night they are allowed to make 2 class changes. This worked in most circumstances but sometimes I would make exceptions to this rule on an individual basis.

The main idea is that the campers have the opportunity to choose their own path when it comes to activities. This gives them ownership in their camp experience.

THE BIG BOARD

After seeing a story about a chalkboard style wall that was created on the side of an abandoned building in New Orleans, we decided to do something similar.

The board had the words "Before I Die..." in large writing with a bunch of lines for people to write their "answers" with sidewalk chalk. Each line started with "Before I die I want to ____".

The board was taken down after someone had bought the property but then similar boards started popping up all over the world.

Our board was placed on the side of our dining hall. Instead of the words "Before I Die..." our board says "Camp Is Special To Me Because..." Campers and staff can write their answers, or read what others wrote, during free time.

It's amazing and touching to see what is written on the board. Each session we take a photo of the board before erasing it in preparation for the next session.

For instructions on how to build your own wall visit the following website - beforeidie.cc/site/build-your-own-before-i-die-wall

GETTIN' 'EM ON THE DANCE FLOOR

I work for a fraternal insurance company. We take our youth to camp each year. In the last few years we have noticed that a lot of the dance hall crowds have become smaller and smaller - especially our younger people.

This last year we taught our teens the Texas Two Step, Polka, Cotton Eye Joe, and a couple of line dances. When we had the dance later that night each time one of the songs that we practiced to played, EVERYONE had to get up and dance. If it was a couple's song I would ring a bell and they would have to quickly change partners.

Everyone had a good time, but the best part was when the teens went back to the youth camps later in the month they were able to help the younger ones learn how to dance. I was out at one of our halls not too long ago and actually saw several of our youth members at the dance - dancing.

As a camp wide activity you could also teach line dancing to disco music. At first the campers might seem hesitant, but soon they will all be having a great time. Just make sure it is not optional. Everyone, including staff, must participate.

At some schools this has become a popular PE activity, so you may find that some of the campers already know the steps.

GOAL BRACELETS
Specific wearable for each group.

All staff and campers were given a strip of fabric that looked like a bandanna (about 1 inch by 10 inches) and a large, natural-colored wooden bead. We talked about making goals for the week with campers, and how the bandanna represented the goal of the whole cabin and every one had a part in it, just as every one had a part of the bandanna.

Each person made a personal goal, which was represented in the bead. Then the bead was put on the strip of bandanna, and worn around our wrists or ankles for the summer. Mine meant so much to me, that I wore it all summer and still have the remains of the faded bracelet and bead!

THE CAMP MONSTER
Spaghetti Steve

A few years back, our counselors, while trying to settle down our youngest campers for the night, decided to tell a story of the friendly camp monster that comes in the night to look for leftover spaghetti. The name of our camp's monster must be protected, so for the purposes of sharing, we'll just call him "Steve". It is important to note that Steve never speaks and is rarely seen (adding to the mystery and the ease of multiple people acting as said monster as staffing/time allows).

So the story goes, Steve found his home at our camp and lives in a hut on the other side of the lake (which isn't camp property, and the young kids will conveniently never go, but they don't know that). He has a dog and a girlfriend, but we've never seen them. We know Steve exists because we sometimes find bits of uncooked spaghetti along the trails and Steve's droppings (melted tootsie rolls with bits of uncooked spaghetti in them. If you've never made fake monster poo in the microwave while sleep deprived on a Thursday at midnight, I highly recommend it).

If the young kids leave some spaghetti treats for Steve, in the morning, the spaghetti will be "eaten" and candy will be left in its place! We also know that Steve has many hiding spots through out camp. While we're on tractor rides between activities, sometimes we see a hairy shadow in the distance running between the trees (the monster costume is a ghillie suit for turkey hunting. While a little pricey, nothing makes a better "swamp monster" costume. He also wears a camp logo bucket hat.)

From his hiding spots, he watches over the kids at camp and sometimes leaves notes for them with the candy, telling them how proud of them he is at how well they played kickball, painted the birdhouse in arts and crafts, or just that he's so glad they tried 3 bites of chicken for dinner, along with the 3 PB&J sandwiches they ate. (The counselors, of course, help Steve write his notes).

Oddly enough, the counselors, even the ones that told the story, never seem to catch a glimpse of Steve. They all know beyond a doubt that he exists, but when the kids see Steve running in the woods, they point and scream, but the counselors never seem to be able to see him. (Egging on 6 year olds in this way is probably more fun for the counselors and frustrating for the kids, but it's all in good fun). The excitement is contagious and it's often hard to settle some of the kids down for hours. I do NOT recommend an evening sighting on the way to the cabins before bedtime. Live and learn...

The kids love the idea of a secret monster friend who watches over them while they are at camp and brings them candy at night. Some, however are NOT ok with the idea of a monster in their cabin while they are sleeping. For this reason, we added a portion of the story where we have found (through scientific research) that Steve is afraid of children's hands! Counselors can easily tell which kids are afraid of monsters (and offer some extra reassurance as necessary) and which kids want to meet him by the way hands immediately become hidden in pockets or become very prominent, waving around as if to scare off some unseen beast. You can also leave the spaghetti on the porch or picnic table outside if even a friendly monster in the cabin is too disagreeable an idea.

Steve creates a whole sub theme in our camp for our young campers. The old campers even get in on the fun by telling their younger siblings even farther flung yarns about Steve's antics in the old kids cabins, or sightings, or what happened when they themselves were in the young cabin, etc.

At some point late in the week, after gathering many stories and "facts" about Steve's habits and whereabouts, our young kids go on a sort of "snipe hunt" for Steve, tracking footprints and spaghetti laden poo around camp, only to end up at the dining hall for dinner JUST as Steve is running out the back door towards his hut across the lake.

Adding a friendly camp monster to your staff can provide practically endless opportunities for activities, themes, sub themes stories and memories. To get things started, my recommendation is that you might want to plant a few green jellybeans in the dirt at your opening campfire... see what kind of fun springs up the next day!

CHOICES and CHALLENGES

We have a day at camp each week that is called choices and challenges, so for this day the campers have an opportunity to sign up for the activity of their choosing instead of doing our regular programs in the morning. We do a random draw of pulling cabin numbers out of a hat and they get to sign up as their cabin is drawn or we sometimes based it on clean cabin criteria working from the cleanest cabin down. There are only so many spots per area so they all anticipate and hope to be one of the first cabins to go.

Below you will see three of the choices and challenges that we have done. Not only is this a day for the campers to do something different but it is a time for staff to do the same and be creative with different activities we normally do not do every week.

PAINTING THE CAMP TRUCK

The truck is old mind you and white so that the paint can easily be seen but the kids love it after all how often can you paint a truck and area of colors and be 100% creative with it, we simply used diluted powder tempera paint.

ALICE IN WONDERLAND TEA PARTY

We started off first by setting up a tea party area in the field with tables, table cloths, benches and decorations to our choosing. The kids meanwhile were picking out their tea party outfits from our tickle trunk. We had fun kid music playing in the background and had a tea party with little sandwiches and actual tea while doing this the campers were able to introduce themselves as their character that they were at the tea party. We than played typical party games from variations of duck, duck, goose; musical chairs and unwrap the parcel to revile a surprise for all of them.

PIONEER CHALLENGE

We have a map of camp that we rip up, or we draw areas of camp from a hat. These are to be the areas that they settle in. Within these areas they need to build a shelter out of nature that is big enough to fit everyone. They need to have an area on the road to build a fire that can cook their bannock. They have to usually come up with a name for their settlement with a flag that they design and then if time permits come up with a game to teach other people that visit their settlement.

A variation of this is to base it around survivor where you would have different survivor challenges for the different tribes to compete against one another. The challenges were much like that of the TV show.

BOX FORTS

At our camp we were able to gather about 70 computer boxes. First thing that came into my mind? Box Forts!!! I took over half the cafeteria and got lots of tape. Then me and about 15 kids built this sweet creation. Before we built the fort I talked about procedures and about why, historically, we build forts.

What You Do Need?
BOXES! Either ask for parents and staff to bring any and all boxes (or cardboard for that matter) or ask for donations from grocery stores or big box stores (Wal-Mart, Kmart, etc.).

Other Supplies You'll Need:
- Tape
- Paper
- Markers
- Scissors or Box Cutters (Only allow the staff to use the latter)
- Imagination

What Do You Do Next?
1. Come up with a design. Do you want an actual fort that will stay up for more than one day or do you want something that looks cool but isn't functional?
2. Next find a perfect location to build your foundation. I would recommend using a "lean-to" concept that way no matter how tall your fort gets, it is still sturdy enough.
3. Start building.
4. Add the finishing details like windows, doors, food storage, spy-towers, etc. The sky (or ceiling) is literally the limit.
5. Enjoy your creation!

Other Resources for Box Forts:
Great article that has pictures and videos of forts...
http://blogs.howstuffworks.com/2010/12/29/box-forts-a-great-thing-for-kids/
The Wikipedia entry for Forts...
http://en.wikipedia.org/wiki/Fortification

Why stop at boxes? Add blankets to the mix:
http://simplemom.net/how-to-build-a-great-blanket-fort/

CABIN AND ME TIME

I am the director of a summer camp where we rent the group camp facilities of a state park. We take all the workers, cooks, staff that is needed along with all the equipment we will need. The program that we have instituted that we really like is the cabin and me time.

One day, at the beginning of the week, a counselor takes their cabin, usually about 7-10 campers, right after breakfast for a three hour time together. During that time, traveling to different parts of this very large state park, they will experience getting back to nature activities, devotions and worship times, one on one with the counselor, hiking, and doing crazy kid stuff in the creeks, at the water falls, or in the woods. It really helps the counselor bond with their campers and when most of them don't know each other very well, the campers bond with each other more. Counselors have become very creative about using the outdoors to get a spiritual and life lesson to the campers.

I really like the idea of counselors getting a large chunk of time to bond with the campers through exploration of the surrounding camp areas. Building these types of relationships (peer-to-peer and mentor-to-mentee) are crucial to changing lives at camp, or at the very least, it is the foundation for creating an awesome camp experience.

During staff training coach your staff through what their Cabin and Me Time would look like. What activities would they do? What conversations would they have? Where will they take their group? Discuss with your staff the purpose of this time away from the main camp.

WHAT EVERY BOY AND GIRL SHOULD KNOW

Kids learn things at camp all the time, how to shoot an arrow, how to ride a horse, how to sail, etc., but there are certain things that all young people should know. Why wait for someone else to teach them, or for them to learn it on their own years later?

Schedule a program that teaches campers things they ought to know. Make sure the tasks are appropriate for the age of the group.

Here is a list of what can be taught...

- How to tie shoes
- How to whistle
- How to give a proper handshake
- Table manners
- How to do laundry
- How to iron
- How to make small talk
- How to build a campfire
- How to properly deliver a joke
- How to shuffle a deck of cards
- How to skip a stone
- The basics about sports
- How to use basic tools
- Basic cooking
- Take a good picture
- Throw a spiral (football)
- How to hand sew a button onto a shirt
- How to use a sewing machine
- Basic first aid
- How to change a bicycle tire
- How to change a car tire

There are a number of books that are available with many more ideas on what boys and girls should know. Imagine what parents will say when they see the knowledge and skills their youngsters have learned at camp.

CAMP DVD

Offering a DVD of camp is one way to ensure that it's unforgettable.

You don't have to video tape everything during the week, session or summer. If you already take pictures just use those. However, try to make sure you get every camper and staff member in at least 2-3 photos.

Next, create a slide show with the pictures and put some music to it. Do not use popular music if you are not paying a royalty fee for it (which can be very expensive) especially if you are selling the DVDs. You can get some great royalty free music collections on Ebay.

Of course, you can also hire a company to do a professional camp video, but that will cost you big bucks and you won't get every camper in the video. Save the professionals for your marketing videos.

Once you have created your slide show with the music, burn it onto a DVD. If your sessions are weekly I suggest having different DVDs for each week. You can either have parents prepay for the DVD during registration, pay for the DVD at the end of the week or add the cost to the registration fee and make sure everyone gets it.

Putting together a slide show with music takes time. Parents will understand when you tell them that the DVD will be shipped out in a few months. That will take the pressure off of you to get it done before they leave, plus, some of the best photo opportunities always happen on the last day of camp.

The other nice thing about sending DVDs out months later is that it is a great reminder to register for the following summer.

CAMP PODCAST

Setting up a podcast system is not complicated. There are many tutorials online that can help you figure out the technical stuff.

Give your campers the opportunity to develop an episode. Divide the campers that are interested into groups of 2 or 3. Help the groups create a 15-30 minute show. Once they are ready they can go into the "podcast room" or area. Show them how everything works. Then hit record and let them go.

Do not let them start over if they make a mistake. Things can be fixed in editing if need be. Personally, I wouldn't worry about editing because it takes so long. Just add an intro and outro and you're done.

Have the podcast activity leader keep note of the episodes that are worthy of being uploaded to your channel on iTunes. You don't want to have to listen to them all at the end of the summer. The best episodes you collect over the summer season can then be played the rest of the year on iTunes. This is a great way to keep kids thinking about camp all year long.

I would have the staff create some episodes as well. Between the camper's episodes and the counselor's episodes you should have enough to play one weekly. you may even have enough to play 2 weekly.

What would the campers (and/or staff) talk about on their episode? Here are some ideas...

- Favorite camp event
- A variety show that includes singing, storytelling and jokes
- What camp means to them
- How they would change camp
- Radio Theater

THE PROGRAM TEAM

In previous summers we had one program (PA, Program Assistant) person for each of our summer programs (Day, Overnight, and High School). We realized that one person was not enough to effectively accomplish all that was needed for each of our summer programs.

This year we implemented a Program Team, which consisted of a Program Supervisor, three Program Assistants, a Media Assistant, and a Music Lead. The team worked together with all of our summer programs to create and execute intentional programming.

Having a team specifically assigned to all of our programs allowed for our programming to go deeper with different and fresh ideas. Instead of being such an independent role, it takes a team effort to bounce ideas back and forth and enhance set ideas. It also took some of the responsibility off of our Overnight and Day Camp Supervisors, so they could focus on making sure the program as a whole is running smoothly.

The Program Media Assistant added a lot of value to our Program Team by enhancing media elements that before were limited to basic IT/AV knowledge. Some examples of this include creating video intros to our evening events, making a daily news show on social media (Facebook) for parents, and being responsible for all IT/AV equipment throughout camp. We realized having one person in charge of all IT/AV equipment kept it organized and in working order.

The Program Team would facilitate morning and evening Rallies (our group gathering times), lead group game times for our Overnight camp, and get to invest in our campers when not planning for Rally or group games.

ACKNOWLEDGMENT

A huge special thanks to all the round table contributors whose submissions were chosen to be in this book.

Abbie P.	Jonathan B.
Alexi B.	Karla D.
Ali M.	Katie L.
Andrea S.	Kaylahree M.
Andy R.	Kevin D.
Baron W.	Kim B.
Becky S.	Kim H.
Bernadette K.	Kim K.
Beverly B.	Kimberly F.
Brenda K.	Kimberly M.
Brent R.	Leah W.
Bri A.	Leigh Ann B.
Carol S.	Lynette N.
Carrie D.	Lynn B.
Carrie M.	Marisa W.
Chelsea S.	Meghan F.
Chris L.	N.T.
Cody T.	Patrick O.
Corina W.	Patti S.
Cory H.	Paula D.
Courtney S.	Philip D.
Daniel G.	Pushpa M.
David B.	Rachael F.
David M.	Randall G.
Debbie N.	Rebecca J.
Denise S.	Rebekah H.
Diane W.	Samantha A.
Dov R.	Sarah H.
Elizabeth S.	Shanelle L.
Emily W.	Shannon B.
Graeme M.	Sherry F.
Holly S.	Siobhan M.
Jacqui M.	Sloan H.
Jacquie L.	Stephanie P.
Janet K.	Terry F.
Janine C.	Thayer R.
Jed B.	Tina M.
Jenn K.	Tink R.
Jennifer M.	Todd G.
Jessica T.	Tory T.
Jill S.	Tricia K.
	Wayne S.